A to Z 神秘案件

中英双语

第一辑

The Absent Author

失踪的作家

SHANGRI-LA HOTEL

[美]罗恩·罗伊 著
[美]约翰·史蒂文·格尼 绘　高芸 译

湖南少年儿童出版社
·长沙·

欢迎来到绿地镇
一起解开 A to Z 神秘案件

北 西 东 南

码头　沿河路

租船处　罗恩鱼饵店　绿地中学　农场路　少女岛
鸭子步行道　老鹰巷　乔希家
绿地小学　林梢鸟道　狐狸小道
银环路　丁丁家　露丝家　牧场路　鹌鹑路
林荫街
宜人街　蓟花街
音乐台　玫瑰园　玫瑰街　野花路
中心公园
天鹅池　绿地高中
运动场　黄杨木巷
体育馆+游泳馆
霍华德理发店
角落书店　清水塘
加油站
奇妙温室　狗舍+兽医
东绿街
镇网球场　儿童游泳池
镇游泳池
镇棒球场　去往蓝山镇
沿河路

人物介绍

三人小组的成员，聪明勇敢，喜欢读推理小说，紧急关头总能保持头脑冷静。喜欢在做事之前好好思考！

丁丁

三人小组的成员，活泼机智，喜欢吃好吃的食物，常常有意想不到的点子。

乔希

三人小组的成员，活泼开朗，喜欢从头到脚穿同一种颜色的衣服，总是那个能找到大部分线索的人。

露丝

著名儿童推理小说作家，未能如约出现在角落书店的签售会现场。

沃利斯·华莱士

角落书店的老板，作家华莱士没有如约出现，他表现得很紧张。

帕斯基先生

自称是一名作家，来见华莱士的，加入了三人小组，和他们一起寻找华莱士。

梅维斯小姐

劳伦斯出租车公司的司机，在机场接到了华莱士，把华莱士送到了香格里拉酒店。

莫琳·希金斯

香格里拉酒店的老板，为作家华莱士办理了入住登记手续。

林克莱特先生

字母 A 代表 absent，缺席……

"快点！"丁丁一边拽着朋友们沿着街道直奔角落书店，一边催促道。

他们累得上气不接下气，透过窗户往里看，店里挤满了孩子，书店的主人帕斯基先生已经摆好了折叠椅。丁丁留意到，大部分椅子上都坐了人。

丁丁看见帕斯基先生坐在一张桌子后面，桌子上有一块白色的大牌子，上面写着：欢迎沃利斯·华莱士！

但是牌子后面的那把椅子上没坐人。丁丁倒吸了一口气，盯着空座位。

沃利斯·华莱士在哪里？

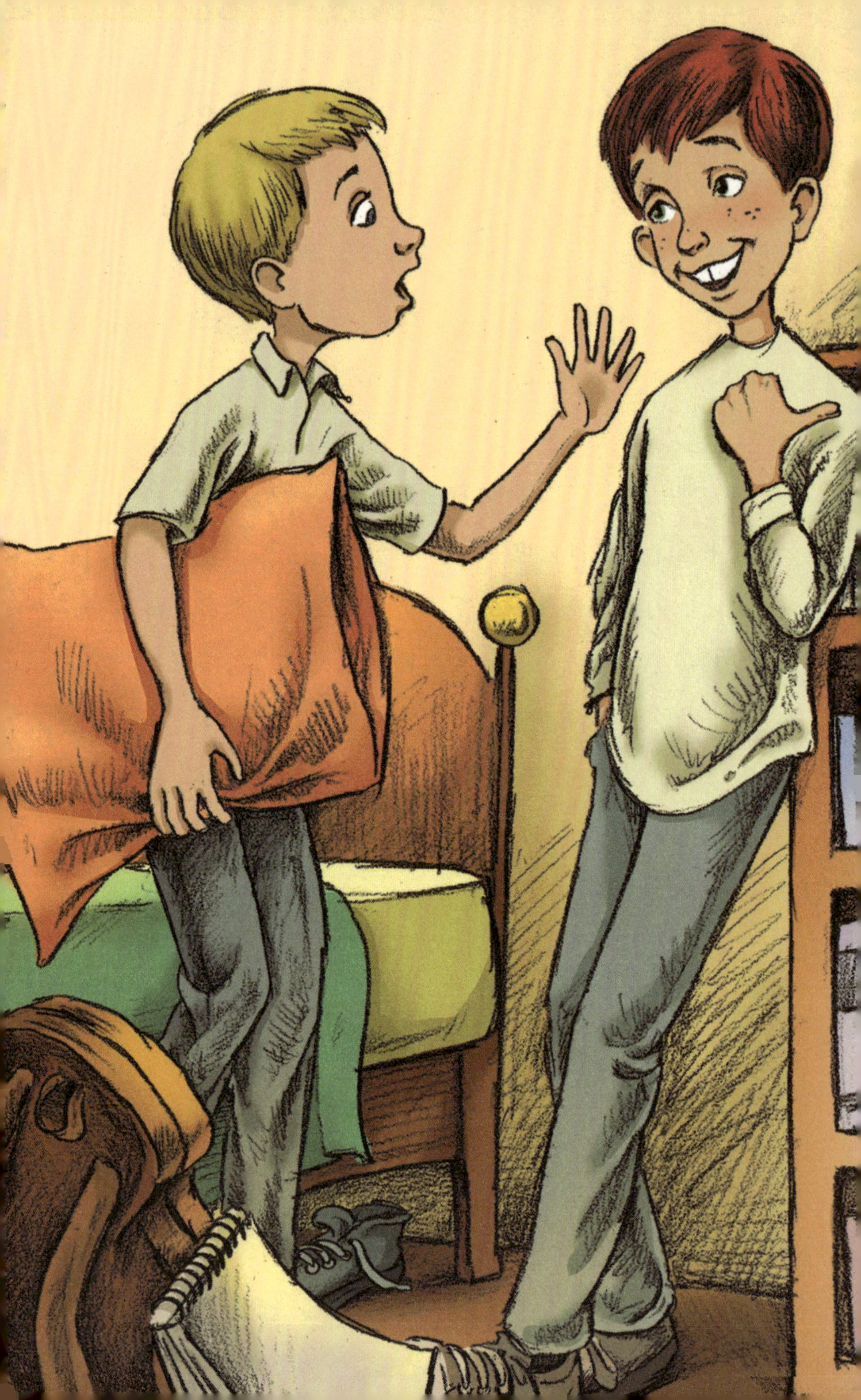

第一章

"求求你了,乔希,"丁丁说,"今天和我一起去吧,就算我欠你一个人情。说吧,你要什么都行!"

丁丁的全名是唐纳德·戴维·邓肯,但是在绿地镇,几乎没有人这样叫他,只有他妈妈动真格的时候,才会如此称呼他。

乔希·平托对着他最好的朋友咧嘴一笑。"要什么都行?"他淘气地抬起那双绿眼睛,看着丁丁卧室的天花板。"让我想想,你有什么我想要的?"他挠了挠头,"我知道了,我要你的宠物洛蕾塔!"

丁丁将枕头扔向乔希。"我说要什么都行,指的是除了我的豚鼠之外,要什么都行!你到底要不要跟我一起去?我必须在十五分钟内赶到角落书店!"

丁丁一边把衬衫塞进牛仔裤里,一边冲进浴室。乔希紧跟其后。

丁丁站在镜子前,用梳子梳了梳浓密的金发。"怎么样?"他问道,"你要和我一起去吗?"

"这个作家有那么重要吗?"乔希坐在浴缸边上问道。

丁丁转过身,用梳子指着乔希说:"沃利斯·华莱士不是普通作家,乔希,他是世界上最著名的推理小说作家!除了你,所有孩子都喜欢读他的书。"

"如果他真的这么著名,为什么他要来小小的绿地镇?"

丁丁冲回卧室,说:"我告诉过你!他之所以来，是因为我邀请了他。要和这么著名的人见面，我害怕得要命。我甚至都不知道该对一个作家说些什么！"

丁丁钻到床底下，拿着运动鞋爬出来。"你愿意陪我一起去吗？"

乔希靠在卧室门口，说："我当然愿意，你这个笨蛋。我只是想让你忐忑不安，平时你可是很淡定的！"

丁丁看着他的朋友："你愿意去？谢谢！我不敢相信沃利斯·华莱士真的会来。我写信邀请他来，可我从没想过他会答应。"

丁丁把背包从壁橱里拽了出来。"把我的书都装进去，好吗？我要让沃利斯·华莱士在所有的书上都签上他的大名！"

乔希开始从丁丁的书架上抽出沃利斯·华莱士的书。"天哪，你究竟有多少本他的书？"

"他写的每一本我都有。"丁丁一边坐在地板上系鞋带，一边说，"到目前为止，一共有二十三本。你真应该读一读它们，乔希。"

乔希选了一本《毒池塘》，看了看封底。

A to Z 神秘案件

"嘿，太酷了！上面写着沃利斯·华莱士住在缅因州的一座城堡里！那不是很棒吗？"

丁丁咧嘴一笑："等我成了著名作家，你可以住在我的城堡里，乔希。"

"得了吧。等我成了著名画家，你可以住在我的城堡里，不过是地下室里！"

乔希又拿起一本《河之谜》。"这个作家长什么样？"他问道，"这些书里怎么都没有他的照片呢？"

"我也感到很奇怪。"丁丁说，"我给他寄了一张我在学校的照片，并向他要了一张他的照片。但他的回信里并没有附照片。"

他系好了鞋带，说："也许沃利斯·华莱士只是不喜欢拍照。"

乔希把二十三本书都塞进了丁丁的背包，并对他咧嘴一笑："也许他太丑了。"

丁丁笑着说："哇，乔希，你也很丑，可是你喜欢拍照。"

"呃……"乔希拿起素描本，"就凭你是我最好的朋友，我要在书店里给他画张像。"

失踪的作家

丁丁看了看手表。"哎呀!"他说,"我们得马上去接露丝·罗斯[1]!"他冲进浴室,开始刷牙。

"你是怎么说服她去的?"乔希喊道。

丁丁冲回房间,擦去嘴上的牙膏。"你在开玩笑吗?露丝喜欢读沃利斯·华莱士的书。"

丁丁把背包一甩,挎在肩上。他和乔希匆匆赶到隔壁——林荫街24号。露丝的橘色猫咪泰格正卧在台阶上晒太阳。

丁丁按了按门铃。

露丝出现在门口。

和往常一样,她从头到脚都穿着同一种颜色的衣服,今天是紫色:紫色衬衫、紫色工装裤和紫色运动鞋,一顶紫色的棒球帽遮住了她的黑色鬈发。

"嘿!"她说着,然后转过身,朝屋里尖声喊道,"我的小伙伴们来了,妈妈。我走啦!"

丁丁和乔希捂住了耳朵。

"天哪,露丝,"乔希说,"你的衣服和声音,不知道哪个更亮堂。"露丝对乔希甜甜一笑。

---

1. 露丝·罗斯在后文简称为露丝。——编者

13

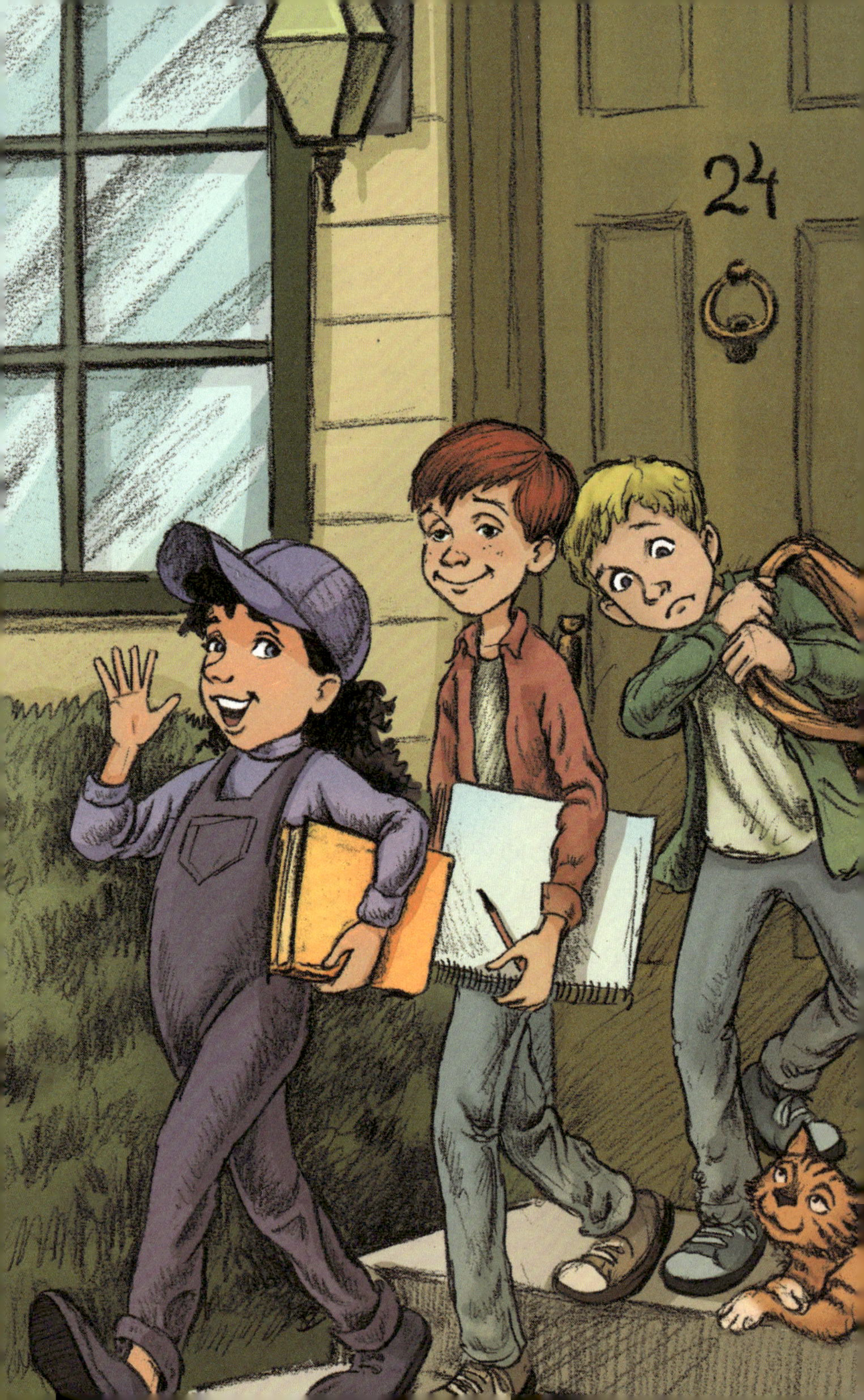
24

"我迫不及待地想让沃利斯·华莱士给我的书签名！"她一边说，一边举起一本《药房里的幽灵》。

"我想知道沃利斯·华莱士会不会朗读他新书里的片段。"丁丁说。

"书名是什么？"露丝问道。

他们朝角落书店走去。

"我不知道，"丁丁说，"但他在信中说，他正在康涅狄格州做调查。"

丁丁从口袋里掏出信，边走边大声念。

亲爱的邓肯先生：

　　谢谢你的来信。你读过我所有的书，这真是让我印象深刻！有个好消息，我已经安排好要去角落书店签名售书，还会抽出部分时间做调查。谢谢你的照片。终于要见到我最忠实的粉丝了，我很高兴。除非被绑架，否则没有什么能阻止我的到来！

　　期待与你早日相见！

沃利斯·华莱士

信上的签名"沃利斯·华莱士"写得很漂亮。丁丁笑着说:"棒极了,是吧?"

"棒极了,邓肯先生!"乔希调侃道。

"你应该把这封信裱起来。"露丝说。

"好主意!"丁丁说。

他们匆匆走过霍华德理发店,霍华德透过窗户向他们挥了挥手。

"快点!"丁丁一边拽着朋友们沿着街道直奔角落书店,一边催促道。

他们累得上气不接下气,透过窗户往里看,店里挤满了孩子,书店的主人帕斯基先生已经摆好了折叠椅。丁丁留意到,大部分椅子上都坐了人。

丁丁看见帕斯基先生坐在一张桌子后面,桌子上有一块白色的大牌子,上面写着:欢迎沃利斯·华莱士!

但是牌子后面的那把椅子上没坐人。丁丁倒吸了一口气,盯着空座位。

沃利斯·华莱士在哪里?

第二章

丁丁冲进角落书店,乔希和露丝紧随其后。他们在汤米·托姆科和埃迪·卡里尼后面找到了三个座位。

丁丁扑通一声把背包扔在地板上,收银台上方的时钟显示是十一点零三分。

"沃利斯·华莱士在哪里?"丁丁轻声问汤米。

汤米转过身说:"这可让你问着了。他还没来,帕斯基先生看起来很焦虑。"

"怎么回事?"露丝问。

丁丁把汤米的话告诉了她和乔希。

"帕斯基先生看起来确实很紧张。"乔希小声说。

"帕斯基先生总是一副紧张兮兮的样子。"丁丁四下观望,轻声回答。他认识的孩子大约有三十个,他的邻居戴维斯太太正在看园艺书。

丁丁看了看店里的其他大人,没有一个看起来像著名的推理小说作家。

帕斯基先生站起来说:"孩子们,欢迎来到角落书店!沃利斯·华莱士随时会到,有多少人想

要他的亲笔签名?"

大家都举起书在空中挥动。

"太棒了!我相信,沃利斯·华莱士如果知道绿地镇的人这么爱读书,一定会很高兴!"

孩子们鼓掌欢呼。

丁丁瞥了一眼时钟,十一点零五分。他咽了口唾沫,努力保持镇静。沃利斯·华莱士迟到了，但只过了五分钟。

又过了缓慢的五分钟，丁丁感到手掌心都在冒汗。"沃利斯·华莱士在哪里？"他思考着。

有些孩子开始变得焦躁不安，丁丁听到有个孩子说："我迟到了就会被罚站！"

"他在哪里？"乔希问。

露丝看了看手表。"才过了十分钟。"她说，"名人总是迟到。"

丁丁盯着时钟。分针猛地向前跳了一格，停顿，然后又向前跳了一格。

十一点十五分，帕斯基先生又站了起来。"我不知道沃利斯·华莱士为什么迟到。"他说。丁丁注意到他不时地拉扯着领结，光秃秃的头上汗水闪闪发光。

帕斯基先生强装笑脸，但是他的眼睛在厚厚的眼镜片后面疯狂地眨着。"我们再等几分钟，好吗？"

大家开始抱怨，但没有人愿意离开。

露丝开始看书。乔希打开素描本，开始给帕斯基先生画像。丁丁转过身，盯着大门，他在心里命令沃利斯·华莱士走进大门。您一定要来！

失踪的作家

丁丁心想。

自从收到沃利斯·华莱士的回信,丁丁只想着一件事:今天和他会面。

突然,丁丁感到心跳加速。那封信!"除非被绑架,"信中写道,"否则没有什么能阻止我的到来!"

绑架!丁丁打了个哆嗦。沃利斯·华莱士当然没有被绑架!

帕斯基先生再次站起身来,但这次他没有笑。"对不起,孩子们,"他说,"看来沃利斯·华莱士是不会来了。"

孩子们不满地嘟囔着。他们站起身来,碰得椅子发出刺耳的嘎吱声,不时地撞到膝盖。他们朝门口挤去,帕斯基先生连声向他们道歉。

"他的每一本书我都读过。"丁丁听到埃米·弗劳尔对另一个女孩说,"我可能再也不会去见任何名人了!"

"真不敢相信,我们为此放弃了一场足球赛!"汤米离开时对埃迪嘀咕道。

露丝和乔希紧跟其后,但丁丁仍然坐在椅子

上。他惊愕得动弹不得。

他隔着牛仔裤口袋摸了摸那封信。"除非被绑架……"最后，丁丁站起身走了出去。

乔希和露丝在等着他。

"怎么了？"露丝说，"你好像有点不舒服！"

"我确实不舒服，"丁丁喃喃地说，"是我邀请他来这儿的，都是我的错。"

"什么都是你的错？"乔希问道。

"这个！"他一边把信猛地塞到乔希手里，一边说，"沃利斯·华莱士被绑架了！"

第三章

"被绑架了?"露丝尖叫道,蓝眼睛睁得大大的。

乔希和丁丁赶紧捂住耳朵。

"嘘!"乔希说着,把信还给丁丁,并迅速地向他们点头示意,"有个陌生女人在看着我们!"

丁丁早就注意到了这个女人,她一直坐在书店的后面。

"她过来了!"露丝说。

这个女人的棕色头发被盘成一个整齐的发

髻，鼻梁上架着一副半框眼镜。她穿着一条棕色的裙子和一双棕色的鞋子，提着一个书包，书包的侧面有一个驼鹿图案。她脖子上围着一条红色的领巾，领巾上面印着许多黑色的小字母。

"请问，"她用柔和而颤抖的声音说，"你们是说沃利斯·华莱士被绑架了吗？"这个女人紧张地推了推眼镜。

丁丁不知道该怎么回答。他觉得沃利斯·华莱士被绑架了，但他不能确定。最后他说："嗯，可能是。"

"我的天哪！"女人倒抽了一口气。

"您是谁？"乔希问她。

"哦，对不起！"女人脸红了。"我叫梅维斯·格林，"她喃喃地说，"我是一名作家，来见华莱士先生的。"

丁丁说："我是丁丁·邓肯，这是我的朋友露丝和乔希。"

梅维斯害羞地和他们握了握手。

然后她把手伸进书包，拿出一张折叠的纸。

"沃利斯·华莱士上周给我来信了，他在信

失踪的作家

中说了一些奇怪的事情。当时我并没有多想。但他今天没有如约而至,而我又听到你们提到绑架……"

她把信递给丁丁,乔希和露丝凑到丁丁的肩头看信。

亲爱的梅维斯:

谢谢你的来信。我很好,谢谢你的关心。但最近我的想象力在捉弄我,我总是觉得有人在跟踪我!也许这就是推理小说作家的通病——我们开始看见暗处的坏人!无论如何,我渴望在绿地镇与你相见,也非常期待签售会后我们共进午餐。

沃利斯·华莱士

A to Z 神秘案件

"哇！"露丝说，"他先是说有人跟踪他，然后就失踪了！"

丁丁也把沃利斯·华莱士给他的回信内容告诉了梅维斯。"沃利斯说除非他被绑架了，否则他一定会出席！"

"哦，天哪！"梅维斯说，"我就是不明白，为什么会有人想绑架沃利斯·华莱士？"

"如果他是世界上最著名的推理小说作家，那他一定很富裕，对吧？"乔希说，"也许有人为了赎金绑架他！"

突然，乔希一把抓住丁丁，让他转过身去，并指着街道说："看！警察来了！他们一定听说了绑架事件！"

一名警官正朝他们走来。

"乔希，那是法伦警官，他是吉米·法伦的爷爷。"丁丁说，"吉米也来找作家签名了，我在书店看见他了。"

"也许我们应该给法伦警官看看这些信。"露丝建议，"如果沃利斯·华莱士真的被绑架了，它们可能就是一些线索！"

失踪的作家

"谁被绑架了？"法伦警官问道，他此时已经站到了他们身旁。"希望不是我的孙子。"他笑着补充道。

丁丁把那两封信拿给法伦警官看。"我们认为沃利斯·华莱士可能被绑架了。"他说，"他答应过要来签名售书，但他没有来。"

法伦警官先读了梅维斯的信，然后读了丁丁的信。他挠了挠下巴，把信还给丁丁。

"这些信确实有点可疑，"他说，"但更有可能的是，华莱士先生只是错过了航班。"

吉米从书店里跑了出来，手里拿着一本沃利斯·华莱士的书，向爷爷挥舞着。"爷爷，他没有来！我们可以去吃冰激凌吗？"

法伦警官把一只大手放在吉米的头上，说："等一下，孩子。"他又对丁丁说："我一点也不担心，华莱士先生会露面的。如果明天还没有消息，你们就给我打电话，好吗？"

他们目送吉米和他的爷爷离开。

丁丁把信还给梅维斯，又把自己的信折好塞进口袋。他的脑海里不断地冒出一些古怪的想

27

法：假如沃利斯·华莱士真的被绑架了怎么办？是因为我邀请他来绿地镇，他才被绑架的。事实上，我就是帮凶！

"我不想等到明天，"他最后说，"我建议我们现在就开始寻找沃利斯·华莱士！"

"我们从哪里开始？"露丝问道。

丁丁猛地把手指举过肩膀，指向身后，说："就在这里，角落书店。"

"请问，"梅维斯害羞地说，"我可以和你们一起去吗？"

"当然可以。"丁丁说。他大步往书店走去，其他人跟在后面。

帕斯基先生正在把沃利斯·华莱士的书放回书架上，他看起来比之前更紧张了。

"打扰一下，帕斯基先生。"丁丁说，"您有沃利斯·华莱士的消息吗？"

帕斯基先生迅速伸手摸了摸领结。"没有，丁丁，一点消息都没有。"

"我们认为他被绑架了！"乔希说。

帕斯基先生咽了口唾沫，拉扯着领结。"好

了,乔希,我们不要草率地下结论。我相信他的缺席一定有一个合理的解释。"

丁丁把两封信的事告诉了帕斯基先生。"我真的很担心,帕斯基先生。他会在哪里呢?"

帕斯基先生掏出一块手帕,擦了擦脸。"我不知道,"他从桌子上拿起一张纸,递给丁丁,"我只有他的行程单。"

沃利斯·华莱士的行程单:

1. 乘坐新英格兰航空公司3132次航班,于7月15日(周五)晚上7:00抵达布拉德利机场。
2. 和劳伦斯出租车公司的司机会合。
3. 乘车前往香格里拉酒店。
4. 7月16日(周六)上午11:00在角落书店签名售书。
5. 吃午餐,然后去机场乘坐下午4:30的航班返回。

A to Z 神秘案件

丁丁看着行程单,其他人都凑到他的肩头一起看。

"我可以留着这张行程单吗?"丁丁问帕斯基先生。

帕斯基先生眨了眨眼睛:"好吧,我想没问题。但你为什么需要行程单呢?"

丁丁拿起一支记号笔,把"机场""出租车""酒店""角落书店"这几个词语圈了起来。

"这就像一条小径,从昨晚的机场一直延伸到今天的书店。"丁丁说,"在这条小径的某个地方,沃利斯·华莱士失踪了。"

丁丁盯着行程单说:"我们会找到他的!"

第四章

帕斯基先生把他们请出书店,锁上前门。"我得吃午餐了。"他说完,沿着主街匆匆而去。

"快点,"丁丁说,"埃莉餐馆里有电话。"

"好的,我们可以趁你打电话的时候吃……"乔希停了下来,"你要给谁打电话?"

"机场。"丁丁说,"问问沃利斯·华莱士昨晚七点是否到达了机场。"

他们走进埃莉餐馆时,吉米和他爷爷正好从里面出来。吉米正在吃三层巧克力甜筒。

埃莉站在柜台后面。和往常一样,她的围裙上沾满了番茄酱、芥末、巧克力,还有很多丁丁

认不出来的东西。

埃莉笑了笑,说:"嘿,丁丁。黄油酥甜筒,对吧?"

丁丁摇了摇头:"不用了,谢谢,埃莉。我是来借用电话的。"

"请问一下,我给你们每人买一个甜筒,可以吗?"梅维斯问道,"我本来打算请华莱士先生

吃午餐的。"

"哇,谢谢。"乔希说,"我要薄荷和开心果口味的双球甜筒。"

"哦,你也喜欢绿色的冰激凌,"梅维斯害羞地笑着说,"我也要一样的,谢谢。"

"我喜欢粉色的冰激凌,"露丝说,"请给我一个单球的草莓甜筒。"

"你呢，丁丁？"梅维斯问道。

"我不饿，谢谢。"他说，"你们吃吧，我要给机场打电话。"

丁丁感到非常内疚。如果他没有邀请沃利斯·华莱士来绿地镇，他最喜欢的作家就会安全地待在缅因州的城堡里。

但丁丁也不禁感到兴奋，他觉得自己就像沃利斯·华莱士小说里的侦探！

丁丁走进公用电话间，查出新英格兰航空公司的电话号码，然后打了过去。电话接通后，他问沃利斯·华莱士昨晚是否在3132次航班上。

"他在？晚上七点钟降落的？"丁丁说道，"非常感谢！"

他冲出电话间："嘿，伙伴们，他们说沃利斯·华莱士在飞机上——而且飞机准点降落了！"

"所以他没有错过航班。"露丝说。她的嘴唇上都是草莓的颜色。

"没错！"丁丁拿出行程单，在"机场"那个词语上画了一条线。

失踪的作家

"这太令人兴奋了!"露丝说。

"现在怎么办?"乔希一边吃着他的双球甜筒,一边问。

丁丁指着行程单上的下一个圆圈。"现在我们需要弄清楚是否有出租车来接他。"他说。

"劳伦斯出租车公司就在河边。"露丝说。

丁丁看着梅维斯:"您愿意和我们一起去吗?只有五分钟的路程。"

梅维斯用餐巾纸小心翼翼地擦了擦嘴唇。"我愿意。"她用柔和的声音说。

他们离开埃莉餐馆,走在大桥路的左侧,然后沿着林景路朝河边走去。

"帕斯基先生看起来相当沮丧,不是吗?"乔希一边吧唧吧唧地吃着最后一个冰激凌球,一边说道。他的下巴都被染绿了。

"如果你的店里有一群顾客等着要见一位著名作家,而他却没有露面,你难道不会感到沮丧吗?"露丝问道。

"会的,但是他流了很多汗。"乔希说,"我在想是不是帕斯基先生绑架了沃利斯·华莱士。"

A to Z 神秘案件

"乔希,现实点吧!为什么帕斯基先生要绑架一个作家?"露丝问道,"他卖了大量沃利斯·华莱士的书!"

"我不认为帕斯基先生是绑架者。"丁丁说,"但在某种程度上,乔希说得对。侦探应该把每个人都视为嫌疑人,就像沃利斯·华莱士的书中所写的那样。"

到了沿河路,他们向左转。两分钟后,丁丁推开了劳伦斯出租车公司办公室的大门。他问柜台后面的人,昨天晚上公司里是否有司机去了布拉德利机场接3132次航班上的客人。

那个人用手指顺着清单上的记录一行行地往下滑。"是莫琳·希金斯。她在外面吃午餐。"他一边指了指后面,一边说,"一直往前走。"

他们穿过大楼,来到后面的一片草地上。透过树林,丁丁可以看到印第安河。太阳反射在水面上,波光粼粼。

一个女人坐在野餐桌旁,一边吃三明治,一边做填字游戏。

"打扰了,请问您是莫琳·希金斯吗?"丁丁

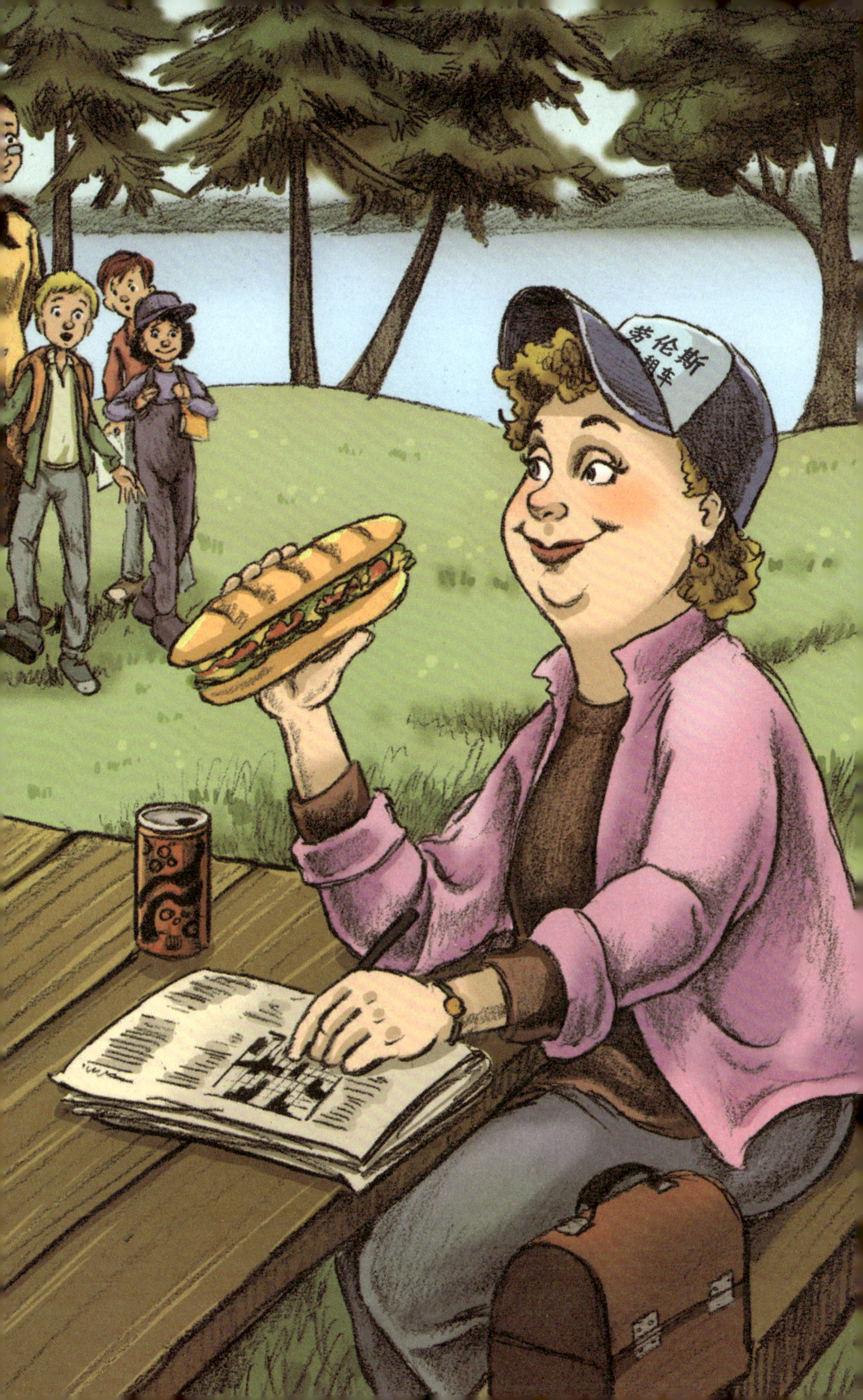
劳伦斯
租车

问道。

这个女人头也没抬就摇了摇头:"不,我是玛丽莲·梦露。"

这个女人又填了一个字母,然后抬起头。她有一双丁丁见过的最漂亮的蓝眼睛。

"是的,小可爱,我是莫琳。"她手拿三明治指着丁丁,问道,"你是谁?"

"我是丁丁·邓肯,"他说,"这是我的朋友乔希、露丝和梅维斯。"

"我们想知道您是否能帮帮我们。"露丝说。

莫琳盯着他们,问道:"怎么帮?"

"昨晚,您有在机场接到一位叫沃利斯·华莱士的客人吗?"丁丁问道。

莫琳眯起一只蓝眼睛,问道:"你为什么想知道这件事?"

"因为他失踪了!"乔希说。

"嗯,我肯定没有绑架他!"莫琳咬了一口三明治,蛋黄酱漏到她的手指上。

"我知道。我的意思是,我们没有认为您绑架了他,"丁丁说,"但是您接到他了吗?"

失踪的作家

莫琳一边点了点头，一边咽下三明治："我当然接到他了。七点整，我就在机场，举着一块牌子，上面写着"华莱士"。这家伙发现了我，小跑过来。我带他出了机场，到了出租车旁，他提着一个小手提箱上了车。这家伙有点怪。他戴着帽子，穿着长雨衣，戴着太阳镜。晚上戴着太阳镜！一句话也不说，只是坐着。真不可思议！"

"您把他送去香格里拉酒店了吗？"丁丁问道。

"是的，这是给我的订单要求。他不需要给我指路，但如果他能说点什么就好了。打发时间嘛，你知道吗？很多人聊天只是为了表示友好，不像这个人这样，安静得像坐在后座上的老鼠。"

莫琳擦去手指和嘴唇上的蛋黄酱，问道："这个叫华莱士的家伙到底是谁？"

"他是一个著名的作家！"露丝说。

莫琳张大了嘴巴："你是说我的车里坐了个名人，而我却浑然不知？"

"你们到达酒店后发生了什么？"乔希问道。

莫琳站了起来，把餐巾纸扔进了垃圾桶。

A to Z 神秘案件

"我下了车,为他打开车门。他跳下车,递给我二十美元,然后迅速地进了大厅,这是我最后一次见到他。"

丁丁拿出行程单,在"出租车"上画了一条粗粗的黑线,然后在"酒店"那个词语旁边画了一个问号。

"非常感谢,希金斯小姐。"他说,"加油,伙伴们,我觉得我们快要找到沃利斯·华莱士了。"

莫琳把手放在丁丁的胳膊上。"我刚想到了一件事,"她说,"这个叫华莱士的家伙把车费递给我时,一直在笑。"

丁丁盯着莫琳:"一直在笑?"

她点了点头:"是的,脸上带着傻笑,好像他知道什么大秘密似的。"

第五章

回到主街上,丁丁调整好背包,领着大家前往香格里拉酒店。

"莫琳说她昨晚把他送到了酒店,"丁丁告诉其他人,"所以我们的下一站是酒店。"

"如果她没有呢?"乔希追上丁丁问。

"你什么意思?"

"我的意思是,也许莫琳没有说实话,也许是她绑架了他!"

"并且把他藏在了午餐盒里!"露丝说。

"真有趣,露丝。"乔希说,"莫琳说她把沃利斯·华莱士送到了酒店,但如果她把他送到了别的地方呢？"

"你可能是对的，"丁丁说，"这就是为什么我们要去酒店。"

在丁丁的带领下，四个人来到酒店大厅的接待处。

"打扰一下。"丁丁对柜台后面的人说。

"我能为您效劳吗？"这个人是丁丁见过的外表最糟糕的人。黑色的头发非常稀疏，眉毛下垂，稀稀拉拉的胡子看起来就像一条睡着的蜈蚣。他的西装外套上别着一个名牌，上面写着：林克莱特。

"我们在找人。"

林克莱特先生盯着丁丁。

"他应该住在这家酒店。"乔希说。

林克莱特先生朝乔希翘了翘胡子。

"他叫沃利斯·华莱士，"丁丁解释道，"您能告诉我们他昨晚是否入住酒店了吗？"

林克莱特先生轻轻地摸着胡子。"年轻人，我们香格里拉酒店有规定。即使有这么一位客人，我们也不会透露他的任何消息。"他声音低沉地说。

"可是他失踪了!"露丝说,"他今天早上本应该出现在角落书店,但是他没有!"

丁丁拿出行程单,说:"看,他是从机场过来的。出租车司机说看见他走进了大厅。"

"而且他很有名!"露丝说着,把书放在林克莱特先生面前的柜台上,"这是他写的书!"

林克莱特先生叹了口气,低头看着露丝:"小姑娘,我们非常清楚华莱士先生是谁。"

林克莱特先生把忧伤的目光转向丁丁。他翻了翻酒店登记簿,瞥了一眼,然后迅速合上。"是的,华莱士先生办理入住了。"他说,"他是八点零五分到达的。"

"是吗?那之后发生了什么?"丁丁问道。

林克莱特先生指着电梯说:"他去了自己的房间。我们提议帮他提箱子,但他宁愿自己提。"

"您今天见到华莱士先生了吗?"梅维斯问道。

"没有,女士,我没有见到他。华莱士先生还在房间里。"

还在房间里!

丁丁突然感到如释重负，还觉得自己有点傻。沃利斯·华莱士根本就没有被绑架，现在他可能就在房间里！

"您能给他打个电话吗？"丁丁问道。

林克莱特先生用手指轻轻地敲了敲合上的登记簿。他捋了捋胡子，眯着眼睛看向丁丁。

"可以吗？"丁丁说，"我们只是想确认他一切都好。"

林克莱特先生终于转过身去，走了几步，拿起一部红色的电话。

他一转身，乔希就抓起了登记簿。乔希很快翻到了昨天的那一页，丁丁和其他人都围拢过去看。

丁丁立刻认出了沃利斯·华莱士的大大的签名，他昨晚八点零五分住进了303号房间。

丁丁拿出沃利斯·华莱士写给他的信，比较了两个签名，它们完全一样。

乔希用胳膊肘碰了一下丁丁。"看！"他小声说。

乔希指着登记簿上的下一行，302号房间也

有人办理入住了，时间是八点十五分。

"在沃利斯·华莱士之后立刻又有人办理入住了！"露丝低声说道。

"但是签名很模糊，"丁丁说，"看不清楚。"

林克莱特先生挂断电话时，乔希立刻推开了登记簿。

林克莱特先生转过身时，丁丁已经合上了登

记簿。丁丁故作天真地抬起头,问道:"他在房间里吗?"

"我不知道。"林克莱特先生用手指轻轻地捋了捋胡子,"无人接听。"

丁丁心里一沉,脑子飞速运转。

如果沃利斯·华莱士昨晚办理入住了,为什么他今天没有出现在书店?

他为什么不接电话?

也许沃利斯·华莱士真的被绑架了!

第六章

丁丁盯着林克莱特先生，问道："无人接听？您确定吗？"

林克莱特先生点点头，他看上去很困惑："也许他在休息，不想被打扰。"

"我们能上去看看吗？"露丝对林克莱特先生甜甜一笑，"这样我们就能确定了。"

林克莱特先生摇了摇头："我们不能打扰客人，小姑娘，香格里拉酒店有规定。再见，谢谢你们。"

露丝张嘴说："但是，林克莱特先……"

"再见。"林克莱特先生再次坚定地说。

丁丁和其他人朝门口走去。

"有点可疑。"丁丁咕哝道。

"是的,"乔希说,"我想是那个叫林克莱特的家伙。你们看到他如何努力隐藏登记簿了吗?然后他又转过身去打电话。也许他根本没有给303号房间打电话,也许他是在给同伙通风报信!"

"你的建议是什么,乔希?"梅维斯问道。

"也许林克莱特先生就是绑匪,"乔希说,"他是最后一个见到沃利斯·华莱士的人。"

一个戴着红帽子的男人轻轻地拍了拍丁丁的肩膀:"打扰一下,我无意中听到你们在谈论我的老板——林克莱特先生,也许我能帮你们找到沃利斯·华莱士。我的孩子们很喜欢他的书。"

"太好了!"丁丁说,"您能带我们进他的房间吗?"

这人摇了摇头:"不能,但我认识今天上午负责打扫三楼房间的服务员,也许她注意到了什么。"

他背对着林克莱特先生,在便笺簿上潦草

地写了几个字,然后把它递给丁丁。"祝你们好运!"那人低声说道,然后匆匆离去。

"他写了什么?"乔希问道。

"到外面说。"丁丁说。

他们连推带挤地过了旋转门。在酒店前面,丁丁看了看那张字条。"服务员名叫莉薇·纽金特,住在橡子公寓4号。"

"莉薇·纽金特?我认识她!"露丝说,"她以前是我的保姆。"

"橡子公寓就在橡树街拐角处,"丁丁说,"我们走吧!"

很快,四个人来到莉薇的家门口,她抱着孩子来开门。一个小孩抱住她的腿,盯着丁丁和其他三个人,脸上和头发上到处都是花生酱。

"嘿,"男孩的妈妈说,"我不买饼干,而且我已经买了《绿地镇报》。"她穿着男式蓝色衬衫和牛仔裤,洋基队棒球帽下露出了棕色头发。

"莉薇,是我!"露丝说。

莉薇盯着露丝,然后咧嘴笑了。

"露丝,你长这么大了!你最近在忙什么?"

"酒店的一位男士让我们来找你。"

"什么人?"

"有点老,戴着一顶红帽子。"丁丁说。

莉薇咯咯地笑了起来:"弗雷迪老吗?他才三十岁!他为什么让你们来找我?"

"他告诉我们,你今天上午打扫了酒店三楼

的房间。"丁丁说,"你打扫303号房间了吗?"

莉薇换了只胳膊抱孩子。"兰迪,不要拽着妈妈的腿。你为什么不去把午餐吃完呢?"兰迪跑回了屋子。

"没有,"莉薇告诉丁丁,"那个房间没人住。我今天上午去的时候,床铺还是叠好的,毛巾也是干燥整洁的。我记得很清楚,因为连着两个房间——303号和302号——我都不必打扫,302号房间的门把手上挂着'请勿打扰'的牌子。所以我很早就回家了,把临时照看孩子的保姆打发走,做好了午餐。"

"但是林克莱特先生告诉我们,沃利斯·华莱士昨晚住进了303号房间。"露丝说。

"不会是推理小说作家沃利斯·华莱士吧?我的小女儿非常喜欢读他的书!"

丁丁点了点头:"今天上午他本应该在角落书店签名售书,但是他一直没有露面!"

"我们甚至在酒店登记簿上看到了他的签名。"露丝说。

"哦,沃利斯·华莱士可能已经办理入住了,但他没在那个房间住过。"莉薇咧嘴一笑,"除非他是个幽灵。"

"我想会不会是林克莱特先生把房间号弄错了。"梅维斯低声提议道。

莉薇朝梅维斯笑了笑,说:"你一定不是本地人,林克莱特先生从来不会出错。"

"所以说沃利斯·华莱士登记入住了,但他没有住在自己的房间里。"丁丁说,"这就意味着……"

"有人在他睡觉前绑架了他!"乔希说。

莉薇的眼睛瞪得大大的。"绑架!天哪,林克莱特先生会大发雷霆的。"她模仿他的声音说,"'我们香格里拉酒店有关于绑架的规定!'。"

除了丁丁,大家都笑了。他满脑子想的都是他最喜欢的作家沃利斯·华莱士被绑架了。

突然,房间里传来了碰撞声。"哎呀,我得赶紧过去,"莉薇说,"兰迪又把妹妹的婴儿车当推土机玩了。我希望你们找到沃利斯·华莱士,如果他不再写书,我的小女儿就活不下去了!"

他们慢慢地走回主街,丁丁觉得他的大脑在

失踪的作家

飞速地运转。

现在他确信,沃利斯·华莱士被绑架了。

但是是谁干的?在什么时候?

沃利斯·华莱士被关在哪里?

"伙伴们,我感到很混乱。"他说,"我们能不能找个地方坐下来,把线索再捋一遍?"

"好主意,"乔希说,"我吃东西的时候,思维总是更敏捷。"

"我也觉得有点饿了。"梅维斯说,"我需要一个人静静地喝杯茶,吃个三明治。我们午餐后再见,好吗?"

露丝看了看手表,说:"我们下午两点钟见吧。"

"在哪里见面?"乔希问道。

"还是在酒店见吧。"丁丁透过大门玻璃凝视着林克莱特先生。

"除非莫琳和林克莱特先生都在撒谎,"他说,"否则沃利斯·华莱士昨晚一定进了香格里拉酒店,而且一直也没有出来。"

第七章

丁丁、乔希和露丝把梅维斯留在埃莉餐馆,然后一起前往丁丁家。丁丁做了金枪鱼三明治和柠檬水,露丝从隔壁自己家里拿来了一袋薯片和一些葡萄干饼干。

他们在丁丁家后院的野餐桌上吃午餐。丁丁咬了一口三明治,咽了下去。他说:"让我们回忆一下了解到的情况。"

他把装柠檬水的玻璃杯移到桌子中间。"我的杯子是机场,"他说,"我们知道沃利斯·华莱士已经到了机场。"

"我们怎么知道他到了?"乔希问道。

"机场告诉我飞机着陆了,乔希。"

"而且莫琳说她接到了他。"露丝补充道。

"好吧,你的杯子就是机场。"乔希说,"继续,丁丁。"

丁丁把装三明治的盘子移到杯子旁边。"我的盘子是莫琳的出租车。"他把一块饼干放到盘子里,"饼干是坐进出租车里的沃利斯·华莱士。"

丁丁把盘子推到打开的薯片袋旁。"这个袋子就是酒店。"他把饼干从盘子里拿出来,放进袋子里。

丁丁看着乔希和露丝说:"但是沃利斯·华莱士走进大厅后发生了什么?"

"我来告诉你发生了什么。"乔希把四块饼干摆成一排说,"这块小饼干是帕斯基先生,这三块是莫琳、林克莱特先生和莉薇。"

乔希抬起头,扬了扬眉毛说:"我认为这四个人一起策划了这次绑架!"

露丝笑了:"乔希,帕斯基先生和莉薇是我们的朋友。你真的认为他们策划了这次绑架吗?你

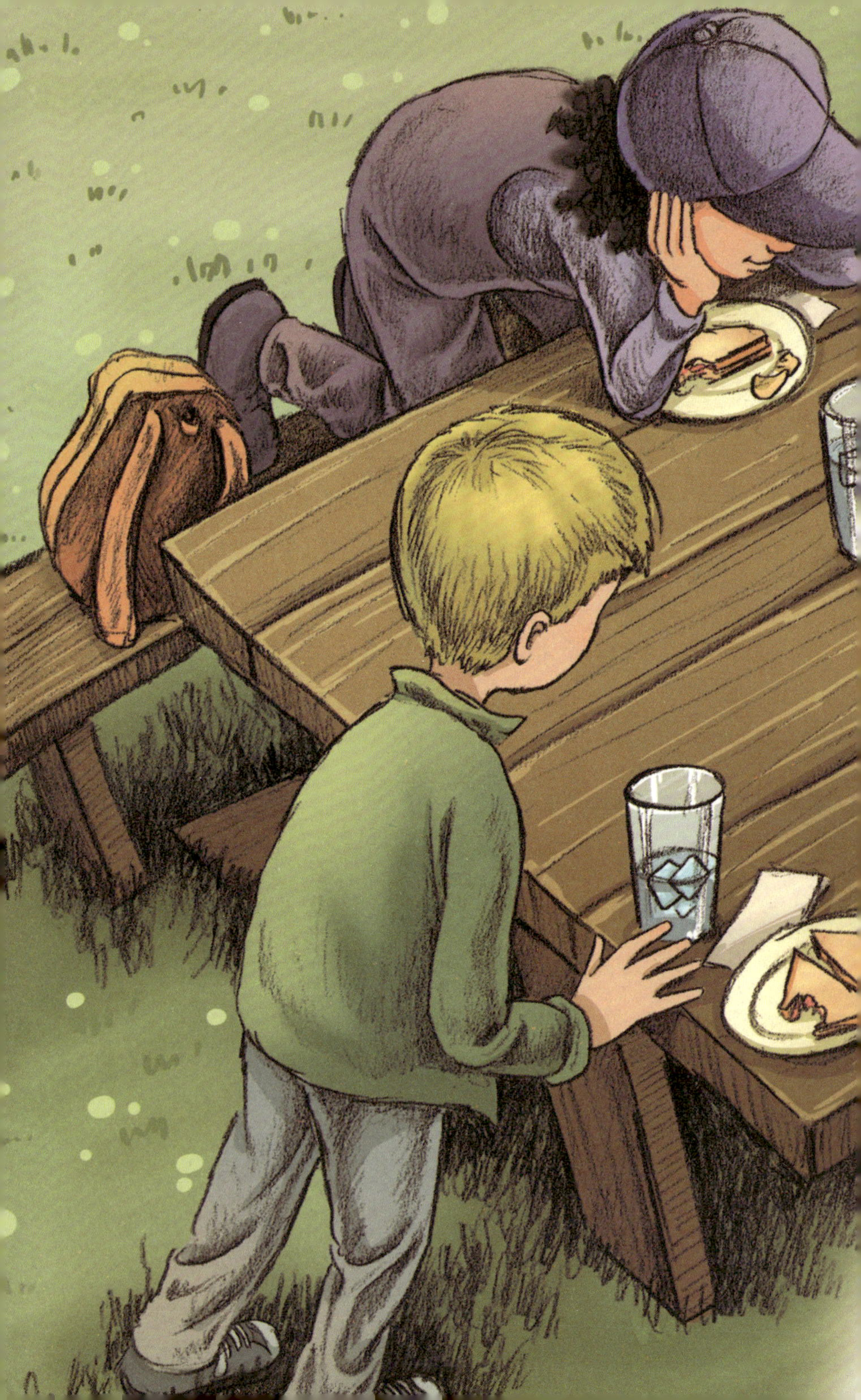

能想象林克莱特先生和我的保姆一起实施绑架？"

乔希吃了一块薯片，说："好吧，也许不是。但是确实有人绑架了那个作家！"

"线索把我们带到了酒店，然后就断了。"丁丁说，"我想知道，如果沃利斯·华莱士不在他的房间，那他在哪里？"

丁丁若有所思地吃着饼干说："想把这一切都弄清楚，我头都疼了。"

露丝翻了翻丁丁的背包，从里面拿出三本沃利斯·华莱士的书。"我有个主意。"她把书递给丁丁和乔希，自己留了一本。

"这些是干什么用的？"丁丁问。

"乔希让我想起了沃利斯·华莱士在《博物馆之谜》中写下的一些话。"露丝说，"他说，对受害人了解得越多，越容易推断出谁是罪犯。"

她翻到书的封底。"所以让我们试着找出更多有关受害人的信息！听听这句话，"她开始大声朗读，"'不写作时，作者喜欢在花园里干活。'理所当然，沃利斯·华莱士最喜欢的颜色是绿色。"

"好吧，"乔希说，"但是知道他最喜欢的颜色，对我们找到他有什么帮助呢，露丝？"

"我不知道，但如果我们多读一些关于他的信息，也许我们就能发现一些线索。"露丝说，"你那本书的封底上写了什么？"

失踪的作家

乔希把书翻过来,开始朗读:"'沃利斯·华莱士住在一座名叫驼鹿庄园的城堡里。'"他抬起头说,"我们早就知道他住在城堡里,我还是没有发现任何线索。"

露丝盯着乔希。"你知道吗?有些事情一直困扰着我,但我不知道是什么,也许是今天某个人说的话。"她摇了摇头说,"不管怎样,读一下你的吧,丁丁。"

丁丁朗读封底的文字:"'沃利斯·华莱士会用写作所得的稿费帮助保护缅因州的野生动物。'"

"好吧,他捐钱保护野生动物,住在城堡里,还种了一堆绿色的植物。"乔希数着手指说道,"但还是没有线索。"

乔希又拿了一块饼干,说:"但我刚刚想到了一些事情。"他开始慢慢地嚼着饼干。

丁丁扬起眉毛说:"你打算告诉我们吗,乔希?"

"嗯,我在想302号房间。你们记得吗?沃利斯·华莱士住进303号房间后,马上有人在登记簿上签了名,住进了302号房间,而且签名模糊不清。然后莉薇——"

"告诉我们302号房间的门把手上挂着'请勿打扰'的牌子!"露丝插嘴说,"莉薇根本就没有进过那个房间!"

就在这时,丁丁的妈妈开车回来了。她下了车,挥了挥手,朝野餐桌走来。

"哦,不!"丁丁说,"如果妈妈发现我在找绑匪,她不会让我出门的!什么都别说,好吗?"

"连打个招呼都不行吗?"乔希问道。

丁丁朝乔希扔了片薯片:"打个招呼,但别说那件事!"

"您好,邓肯太太!"乔希一边说,一边瞥了丁丁一眼。

"嘿,孩子们。签售会怎么样?跟我说说沃利斯·华莱士吧,丁丁,他和你想象的一样了不起吗?"

丁丁盯着妈妈。他不想撒谎,但如果他告诉她真相,她就不会让他继续寻找沃利斯·华莱士。丁丁突然觉得他们很快就能找到他了。

我们现在不能停止!他想。他看着妈妈,傻

乎乎地咧着嘴笑。

"丁丁？宝贝？你的嘴怎么张得那么大？"

他闭上嘴。快想想办法，丁丁！他命令自己。

突然，乔希打翻了他的装着柠檬水的玻璃杯，黏糊糊的冰冷液体洒到了丁丁的腿上。

丁丁大叫一声，跳了起来。

"哎呀，对不起！"乔希说。

"纸巾！"丁丁的妈妈朝屋里跑去。

"聪明极了，乔希。"丁丁一边说，一边擦着湿漉漉的牛仔裤，"但你非得洒到我身上吗？整个院子你都可以洒！"

乔希笑着说："有些人永远不会知足。我把你从水深火热中解救出来了，不是吗？"

"然后直接掉进冰凉的柠檬水里。"露丝说。

丁丁用一沓餐巾纸吸干了牛仔裤上的水。"快点，在我妈妈出来之前，我们去跟梅维斯碰头吧。香格里拉酒店的三楼发生了一些怪事！"

61

第八章

他们到达酒店时,丁丁的牛仔裤差不多干了。梅维斯正在门外等着。

"你们的午餐吃得怎么样?"她怯生生地问道。

"很好,谢谢。"丁丁说,"我们讨论过了,认为这家酒店的三楼有点可疑。"

梅维斯突然开始咳嗽,掀起领巾遮住嘴巴。

丁丁注意到领巾上的字母是小小的 M。"您没事吧?"他问。

"我跑进去给您拿杯水,好吗?"乔希问道。

梅维斯摘下眼镜,摇了摇头:"不用,我很好,谢谢你们。天哪,我不知道发生了什么事!

失踪的作家

嗯,你刚才说三楼什么来着?"

"我们认为沃利斯·华莱士可能就在那里。"露丝说。她提醒梅维斯,302号房间的客人的签名模糊不清,以及门上挂着"请勿打扰"的牌子。

梅维斯重新戴上眼镜。"哎呀!你们觉得我们该怎么办?"

"跟我来!"丁丁说道。他们再一次成群结队地走进酒店大厅。

林克莱特先生从柜台后面看着他们。

"您好,"丁丁说,"还记得我们吗?"

"记忆犹新。"林克莱特先生说。

"沃利斯·华莱士入住了303号房间,对吧?"

"没错。"林克莱特先生说。

"嗯,我们问过了打扫房间的服务员,"丁丁继续说,"她告诉我们没有人在那个房间住过。"

"你们问过莉薇了?什么时候?怎么问的?"

"我们有自己的方法。"乔希说。

"所以,"丁丁接着说,"我们认为沃利斯·华莱士就是在这家酒店失踪的。"

"沃利斯·华莱士是一位非常著名的作家。"

63

露丝提醒林克莱特先生。"数百万名孩子都在期待他的下一部作品。"她甜甜地补充道。

林克莱特先生忧伤的眼睛瞪得大大的。他咽了口唾沫,喉结上下滚动。他又揉了揉额头,好像头痛似的。

接着,丁丁告诉林克莱特先生302号房间的情况:"莉薇说门上有个'请勿打扰'的牌子。"

露丝指着登记簿说:"看到了吗?这个签名都看不清楚!"

"我们认为绑匪把沃利斯·华莱士藏在了那个房间里!"乔希说。

失踪的作家

听到"绑匪"二字，林克莱特先生闭上了眼睛。他打开抽屉，拿出一瓶头痛药，取出一片放进嘴里。

"为了安全起见，也许我们应该检查一下这两个房间，林克莱特先生。"梅维斯轻声地说。

A to Z 神秘案件

"只需要几分钟。"丁丁说。

林克莱特先生重重地叹了口气:"好的,但这极不寻常。香格里拉酒店一直都很太平。"

他们一起进了电梯,没有一个人说话。丁丁看着林克莱特先生摇晃着一串钥匙,林克莱特先生目不转睛地盯着那个显示楼层的小箭头。

电梯门在三楼打开了,林克莱特先生打开了303号房间的门。"极不寻常。"他喃喃自语。

房间里空无一人,干干净净。"奇怪,非常奇怪。"林克莱特先生说。

他们来到302号房间门口,"请勿打扰"的牌子仍挂在门把手上。

林克莱特先生敲了敲房门,他们都向门口靠去。

"听,我听到有人在说话!"乔希说。

"说什么?"露丝问道。

接着,他们都听到了。

那声音很低沉,但确确实实是在喊"救命"。

第九章

林克莱特先生开了锁，把门推开。

一个金色鬈发的男人回过头来盯着他们。他坐在椅子上，双脚被绑在身前，双臂被绑在背后，嘴巴上缠着一条毛巾。

"哦，我的天哪！"林克莱特先生喊道。

大家冲进房间。

丁丁跑到椅子后面，松开那个人的手，乔希松开了他的脚。

梅维斯解开了缠在他脸上的毛巾。

"幸亏你们来了！"这人说道，"我是沃利斯·华莱士。昨晚有人敲门，说他是客房服务部

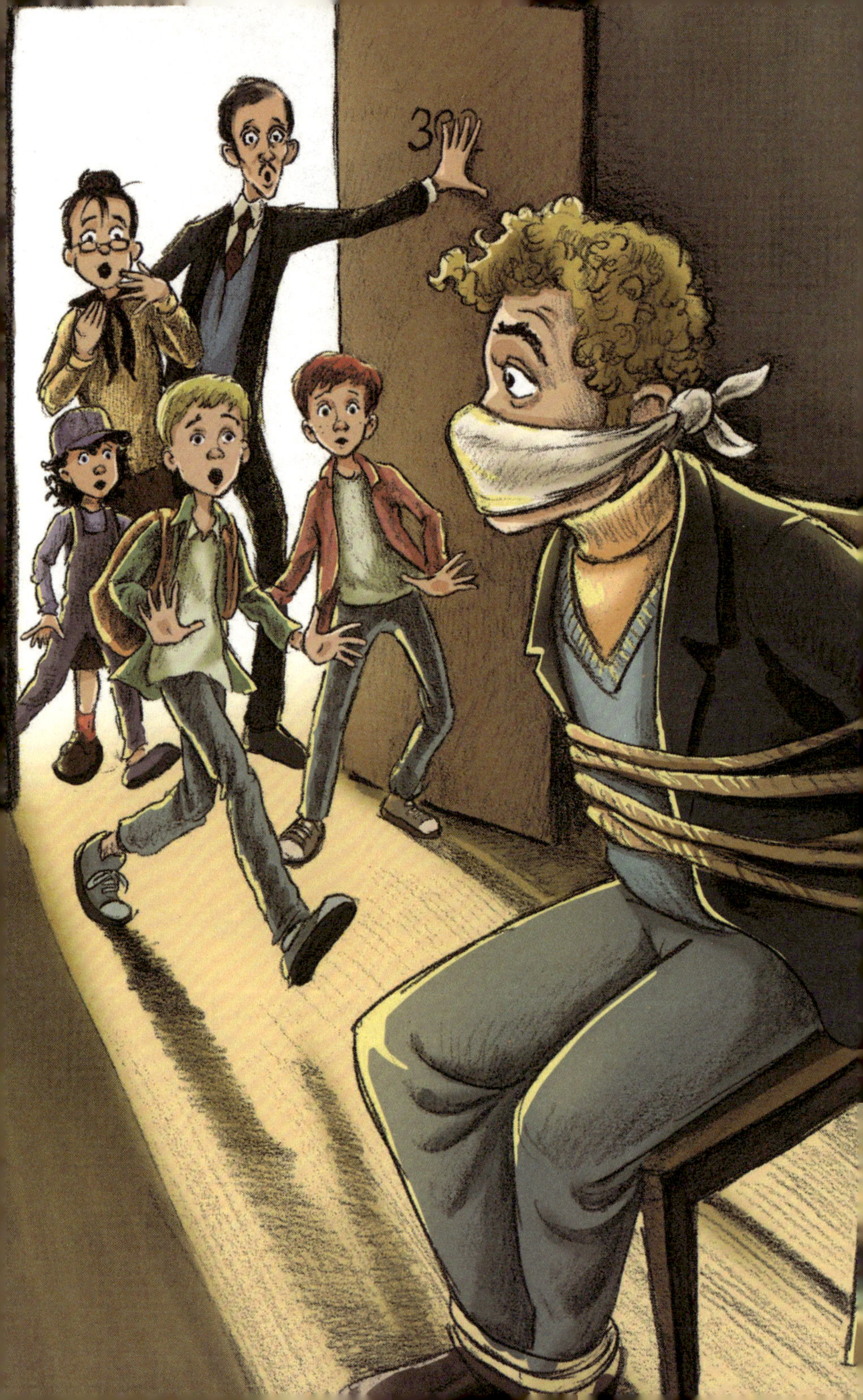

的。当我打开门后,两个男人把我拖到这里,绑了起来。"

他看向丁丁:"你是丁丁·邓肯!我看过你的照片,我认得你。你是怎么找到我的?"

"根据您的行程。"丁丁说着,给华莱士先生看了那张行程单,"我们从帕斯基先生那里拿到了它,它是一个线索,将我们带到了这个房间!"

"很抱歉,我错过了签售会。"沃利斯·华莱士说,"正如你们亲眼所见,我被绑起来了。"

他笑着,揉了揉下巴说:"毛巾把我的嘴巴都弄疼了,真不敢相信我被绑架了!我迫不及待地想回到缅因州的安全小屋。"

"您能描述一下绑架您的那两个家伙吗?"丁丁问道,"我们将告诉法伦警官,让他设法找到他们。"

沃利斯·华莱士盯着丁丁说:"那两个家伙?哦……嗯,嗯,我认为我不会……"

"嘿!"露丝突然喊道。

大家都看着她。

"怎么啦?"丁丁问道,"你看起来怪怪的,露丝。"

露丝盯着梅维斯脖子上的红色领巾,指着那个之前被捆绑起来的人说:"你不是沃利斯·华莱士!"

然后她看向梅维斯。"您才是。"她轻声说。

第十章

"露丝,你在说什么?"乔希说。

丁丁脑子里一片空白,只觉得头疼。

"你凭什么认为我是沃利斯·华莱士?"梅维斯问道。

露丝走到梅维斯身边。"我可以借用一下您的领巾吗?"她说。

露丝把领巾举起来,让每个人都能看到。"第一次看到这条领巾时,我以为这些小小的黑色字母是M,"她说,"M代表梅维斯[1]。"

---

[1] 梅维斯的英文是Mavis,M是Mavis的首字母,所以露丝认为M代表梅维斯。——译者

A to Z 神秘案件

她看着梅维斯问:"但它们不是 M,对吗?"

她把领巾完全颠倒过来,问道:"它们现在看上去像什么?"

丁丁走近了一些,说:"它们现在是小小的 W 了!"

"对,W 代表沃利斯·华莱士![1]"露丝指着那个人说,"你刚才说,你住在一间小屋里,但沃利斯·华莱士住在缅因州的一座大城堡里,《寂静的沼泽》的封底上是这么写的。"

露丝指着梅维斯的书包:"再次看到您的包,让我想起了今天一直困扰我的一些事情。乔希从书上了解到您住的城堡叫作驼鹿庄园,而您的书包上有驼鹿的图案。"

露丝把领巾还给梅维斯:"我们还在书上读到沃利斯·华莱士最喜欢的颜色是绿色。您喜欢绿色冰激凌,所以选择梅维斯·格林作为您的

1.沃利斯·华莱士的英文是 Wallis Wallace,W 是 Wallis 和 Wallace 的首字母,所以露丝认为 W 代表沃利斯·华莱士。——译者

假名。[1]"

除了那个被松绑的男人,每个人都盯着露丝。然后那个男人笑了起来。

"妹妹,秘密已经被发现啦。"他说。

梅维斯笑了,拥抱了露丝一下。

"是的,露丝。"梅维斯说,"我的确是沃利斯·华莱士。"她把手放在那个男人的肩膀上,"这是我哥哥,沃克·华莱士。这次'绑架',我们已经策划了好几周了!"

丁丁盯着梅维斯,或者别的什么人。"您是说沃利斯·华莱士是个女人?"他问。

"是的,丁丁,我是女人,我确确实实是沃利斯·华莱士。"她冲他眨了眨眼说,"真的!"

梅维斯,真正的沃利斯·华莱士,在床上坐了下来。她摘下眼镜,取下头上的发夹,甩了甩头发,一头蓬松的鬈发披散下来。

"谢天谢地,我现在可以做我自己了!"她说,"一整天我都在做胆小的梅维斯。我迫不及

---

1. 格林的英文是 Green,意为绿色。——译者

待地想脱下这条古板的裙子，穿上牛仔裤！"

她踢掉鞋子，摆动着脚趾："哇！这感觉真是太好了！"

丁丁眨了眨眼睛，摇了摇头。梅维斯·格林真的是沃利斯·华莱士？他简直不敢相信。"但您为什么要假装被绑架呢？"他问道。

真正的沃利斯·华莱士对着惊讶的孩子们咧嘴一笑。"我欠你们一个解释。"她说。

"我的新书是关于一位儿童推理小说作家被绑架的故事。书中孩子们营救了这位作家,我想知道现实中的孩子们会如何解开这个谜团。"她解释道。

她对着丁丁笑了笑:"那时你正好给我来信,邀请我来绿地镇,这让我产生了假装自己被绑架的想法。我变成了梅维斯,观察发生的一切。"

"哦,是啊!"丁丁说,"您在信中说,您正在康涅狄格州做调查。"

她点了点头。"是的,我特意在信中提到'绑架'一词,想让你沿着这个思路思考。"她对三个孩子笑了笑,"我还以为需要给你们更多的线索呢,但你们自己解开了这个谜团!"

丁丁笑了。"根据我的照片,您在书店里认出了我。"他说,"而您却没有给我寄照片,这样我就认不出您了!"

"然后我古怪的妹妹把我拉入了她的计划,"沃克·华莱士说,"我这会儿本应该在家检查捕虾笼。"

"你们吃午餐的时候,沃克和我就在这里吃午餐。"沃利斯说,"然后,快两点了,我把他绑在椅子上,跑到楼下,以梅维斯的身份在门外与你们见面。"

沃利斯·华莱士仰头大笑:"你们还记得丁丁在楼下说三楼有点可疑吗?"

她起身站在她哥哥旁边:"嗯,我总是取笑沃克,说他摆弄龙虾诱饵时身上有股鱼腥味。所以当你说酒店里有点可疑的时候,我不得不假装咳嗽，这样你们就不知道我其实是在笑！[1]"

"天哪，您把我们耍得团团转。"丁丁说。

沃利斯·华莱士咧嘴一笑："帕斯基先生也参与其中了，我必须告诉他实情。正如你们今天上午在书店所看到的，我的小小计划让他非常紧张。我答应过他，我很快就会回来办一场真正的签售会。不过我还是会乔装打扮，所以你们要做好准备！"

丁丁摇了摇头。"上午没能见到最喜欢的作家，我非常失望。"他说，"然而，一整天都和您在一起，我却一点都没有察觉！"

她看着丁丁："非常抱歉，我欺骗了你。你能原谅我吗？"

丁丁红着脸说："当然。"

"我有一个问题，"乔希说，"您昨晚到底住在哪里？"

"就在这里，302号房间。几周前，我打

---

[1] 英语中 fishy 的意思是可疑的，有鱼腥味的。"Something was fishy in the hotel"的字面意思有两种：一种是酒店里有点可疑，另一种是酒店里有股鱼腥味。——译者

电话预订了两个相邻的房间。昨晚,我以沃利斯·华莱士的身份住进了303号房间。到了房间后,我摘下帽子,脱了外套,取下太阳镜,然后戴着金色假发偷偷溜回大厅。我再次登记入住,这次是302房间。"

"您弄花了签名吗?"露丝问道。

"哦,你注意到了!"沃利斯说,"我习惯在书上签我的真名,一开始就写了'沃利斯',所以我'不小心'把签名弄花了。"

"我有个问题,梅维斯,我是指华莱士小姐……我们该怎么称呼您呢?"丁丁问道。

"朋友们都叫我沃利斯。"她说。

"哦,出租车司机告诉我们,您在出租车上一直在笑。您在笑什么呢?"

沃利斯·华莱士忍不住又笑了:"哦,有很多好笑的事情。首先,我伪装成男人,这让我觉得有点可笑。其次,我知道我会见到你,我最忠实的粉丝。还有,让我非常高兴的是,我知道无论发生什么,第二天都会很有趣!"

"我确实觉得很有趣,"乔希笑着说,"可怜的帕斯基先生，不得不板着脸对所有人撒谎！"

"天哪，我今天一整天都在假装梅维斯，可真不容易。"沃利斯说，"但我的计划成功了，我遇到了三位出色的侦探。你们让我了解到现实中的孩子是如何调查绑架案的，现在我可以回缅因州完成这部推理小说了。"

"为什么您的书籍封套上从来不写您是女人呢？"露丝问道。

沃利斯·华莱士笑了。"因为我的名字，大多数人都以为我是男人。"她解释道，"我让他们保持这种想法，这样我就可以更容易地进行调查。我很清楚，如果大家知道我是沃利斯·华莱士，他们就会保持沉默。所以在公共场合，我假装自己是梅维斯，一个普通人，而不是推理小说作家。"

"我明白了！"丁丁说，"所以书里没有您的照片，这样就没有人能认出您。"

"对。我希望你们能保守我的秘密。"

"我们会的。对吧，伙伴们？"露丝说。

"谢谢！还有什么问题吗？"沃利斯问道。

A to Z 神秘案件

"得了吧,"沃克一边说,一边看了看妹妹,"我们什么时候离开?还有龙虾在等着我呢。"

"我也有一个问题,"丁丁说,"现在可以把您的照片给我一张吗?"

"可以,我还可以做得更多。"沃利斯说,"我要把新书献给我的三个新朋友。"

丁丁、乔希和露丝三人击掌庆祝。

失踪的作家

"打扰一下。"林克莱特先生说道。他一直站在门口。

大家都看向他。

"快到结账退房的时间了。"

大家都笑了起来。

林克莱特先生也笑了,但只是微微笑了一下。

A to Z Mysteries®

THE ABSENT AUTHOR

by Ron Roy

illustrated by
John Steven Gurney

INDIAN RIVER
LAWRENCE TAXI
RIVER ROAD
HORSE TRAILS
HORSES FOR RENT
BIKE PATH
WOODS
BIKE PATH
WOODVIEW ROAD
INDIAN WAY ROAD
FIRE STATION
BILL'S BIKES
SUPER MARKET
BRIDGE LANE
ROBIN ROAD
CROW ST
FINCH LA
THRUSH CT
OWL RD
PHEASANT LA
BLUE JAY WAY
WREN DR
FITNESS CENTER
WOODS
BIKE PATH
BLUE BIRD WAY
HUMMINGBIRD LA
WOODCOCK CROSS
ELLIE'S DINER
ACORN APTS
FURRY FEET PET SHOP
OAK STREET
BIKE PATH
CENTER CHURCH
PEOPLE'S POND
POST OFFICE
COMMUNITY GARDEN AND FISH POND
GREEN LAWN $ SAVINGS $ BANK
ELDERLY HOUSING
POLICE STATION
WEST GREEN ST
GOOSE ISLAND
RIVER ROAD
GREEN LAWN LIBRARY
SENIOR COMMUNITY CENTER
TOWN HALL
MAIN STREET
BIKE PATH
CHILDREN'S PETTING ZOO AND AQUARIUM
SHANGRI-LA HOTEL

WELCOME TO
GREEN LAWN
HOME OF THE
A to Z Mysteries
N
W
E
S
RIVER ROAD
BOAT LAUNCH
SQUAW ISLAND
BOAT RENTAL
RON'S BAIT
DUCK WALK WAY
GREEN LAWN MIDDLE SCHOOL
EAGLE LANE
FARM LANE
JOSH
GREEN LAWN ELEMENTARY SCHOOL
DINK
RUTH ROSE
TREE TOP CIRCLE
MEADOW ROAD
FOX LANE
QUAIL RUN ROAD
SILVER CIRCLE
WOODY STREET
PLEASANT STREET
THISTLE COURT
WILDFLOWER WAY
BAND SHELL
ROSE GARDEN
CENTER PARK
ROSE STREET
SWAN POND
GREEN LAWN HIGH SCHOOL
PLAYING FIELDS
GYM + POOL
BOXWOOD LANE
HOWARD'S BARBER-SHOP
BOOK NOOK
GAS STATION
CRYSTAL POND
MYSTIC GREENHOUSE
DOG KENNEL + VETERINARIAN
RIVER ROAD
EAST GREEN STREET
TOWN TENNIS COURTS
TOWN SWIMMING POOL
KIDDIE POOL
TOWN BASEBALL FIELD
TO THE BLUE HILLS

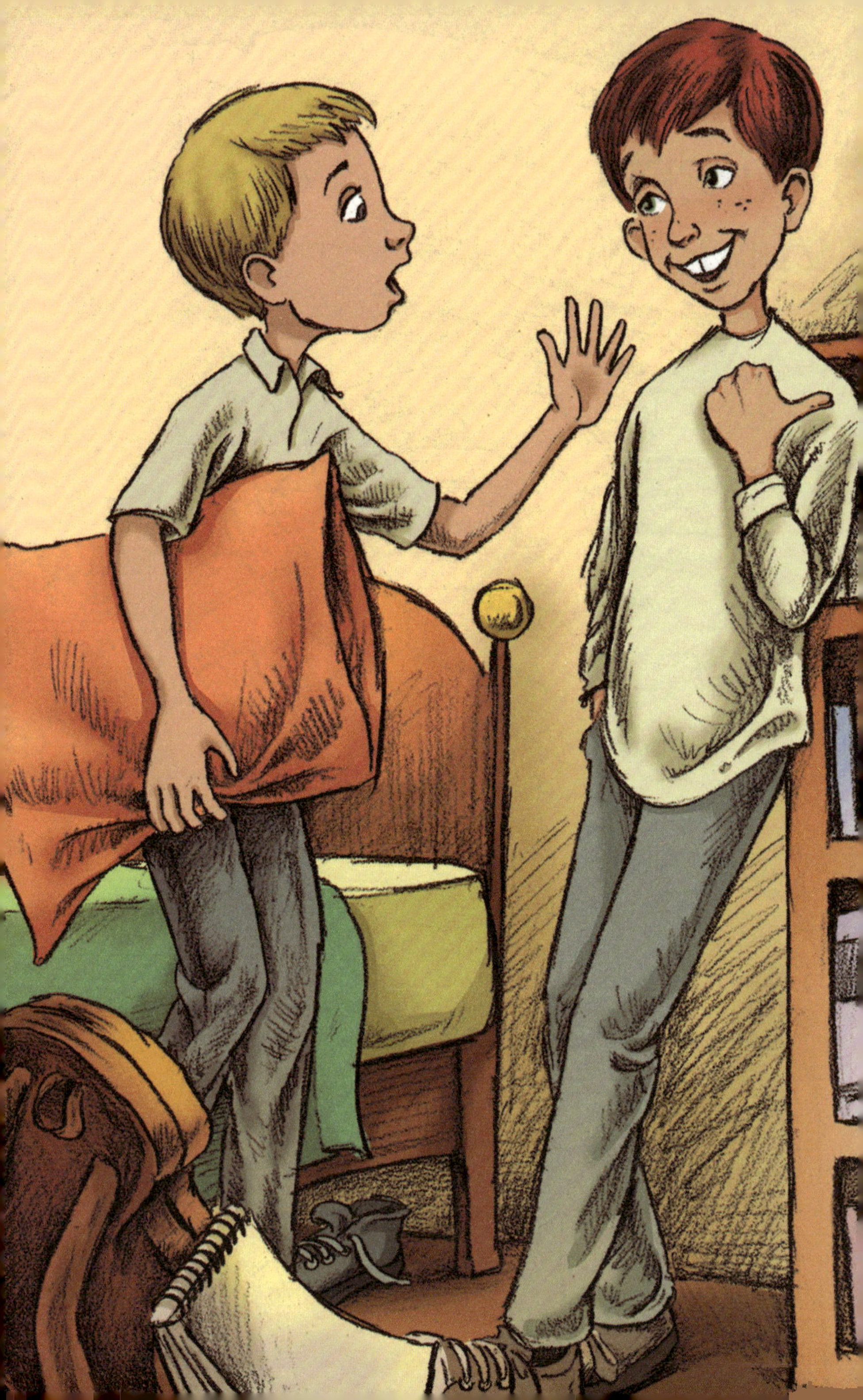

Chapter 1

"Please, Josh," Dink said. "If you come with me today, I'll owe you one. Just name it. Anything!"

Dink's full name was Donald David Duncan. But no one in Green Lawn ever called him that. Except his mother, when she meant business.

Josh Pinto grinned at his best friend.

"Anything?" He raised his mischievous green eyes toward the ceiling of Dink's bedroom. "Let's see, what do you have that I want?" He scratched his head. "I know, I'll take Loretta!"

Dink tossed a pillow at Josh. "When I said anything, I meant anything but my guinea pig! Are you coming with me or not? I have to be at the Book Nook in fifteen minutes!"

Dink rushed into the bathroom, tucking his shirt into his jeans at the same time. Josh followed him.

Standing in front of the mirror, Dink yanked a brush through his thick blond hair. "Well?" he asked. "Are you coming with me?"

"What's so important about this writer guy?" Josh asked, sitting on the edge of the bathtub.

Dink turned around and pointed his hairbrush. "Wallis Wallace isn't just some writer guy, Josh. He's the most famous mystery writer in the world! All the kids read his books. Except for you."

"If he's so famous, why's he coming to dinky little Green Lawn?"

Dink charged back into his bedroom. "I told you! He's coming because I invited him. I'm scared to death to meet someone so famous. I don't even know what you're supposed to say to an author!"

Dink dived under his bed and backed out again with his sneakers. "Please come with me?"

Josh leaned in the bedroom doorway. "Sure I'll come, you dope. I'm just trying to make you sweat. Usually you're so calm!"

Dink stared at his friend. "You will? Thanks! I can't believe Wallis Wallace is really coming. When I wrote and asked him, I never thought he'd say yes."

Dink yanked his backpack out of his closet. "Pack my books, okay? I'm getting Wallis Wallace to sign them all!"

Josh began pulling Wallis Wallace books off Dink's bookshelf. "Geez, how many do you have?"

"Every one he's written." Dink sat on the floor to tie his sneakers. "Twenty-three so far. You should read some of them, Josh."

Josh picked out *The Poisoned Pond* and read the back cover. "Hey, cool! It says here that Wallis Wallace lives in a castle in Maine! Wouldn't that be neat?"

Dink grinned. "When I'm a famous writer, you can live in my castle, Josh."

"No way. When I'm a famous artist, you can live in my castle. Down in the basement!"

Josh picked up *The Riddle in the River*. "What's this guy look like?" he asked. "And how come his picture isn't on any of these books?"

"I wondered about that, too," Dink said. "I sent him one of my school pictures and asked for one of him. But when I got his letter, there was no picture."

He finished tying his laces. "Maybe Wallis Wallace just doesn't like having his picture taken."

Josh squeezed all twenty-three books into Dink's pack. He grinned at Dink. "Or maybe he's just too ugly."

Dink laughed. "Gee, Josh, you're ugly and you love having your picture taken."

"Haw, haw." Josh picked up his drawing pad. "But just because you're my best friend, I'll draw his picture at the bookstore."

Dink looked at his watch. "Yikes!" he said. "We have to pick up Ruth Rose in one minute!" He tore into the bathroom and started brushing his teeth.

"How'd you get her to come?" Josh called.

失踪的作家

Dink rushed back into his room, wiping toothpaste from his mouth. "You kidding? Ruth Rose loves Wallis Wallace's books."

Dink slung his backpack over his shoulder. He and Josh hurried next door to 24 Woody Street. Tiger, Ruth Rose's orange cat, was sitting in the sun on the steps.

Dink pressed the doorbell.

Ruth Rose showed up at the door.

As usual, she was dressed all in one color. Today it was purple. She wore purple coveralls over a purple shirt and had on purple running shoes. A purple baseball cap kept her black curls out of her face.

"Hey," she said. Then she turned around and screamed into the house. "THE GUYS ARE HERE, MOM. I'M LEAVING!"

Dink and Josh covered their ears.

"Geez, Ruth Rose," Josh said. "I don't know what's louder, your outfit or your voice."

Ruth Rose smiled sweetly at Josh.

"I can't wait until Wallis Wallace signs my book!" she said. She held up a copy of *The Phantom in the*

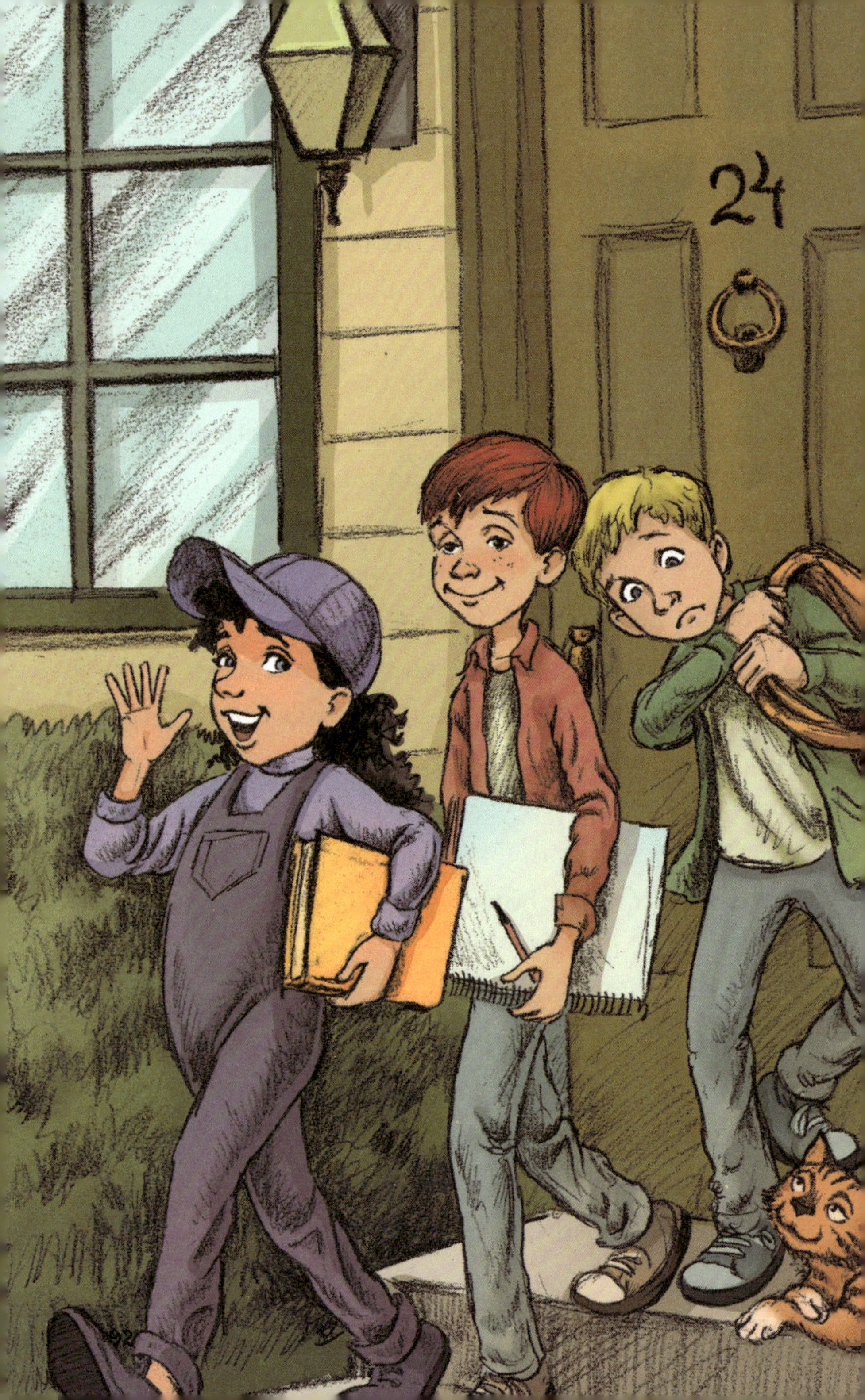
24

Pharmacy.

"I wonder if Wallis Wallace will read from the new book he's working on," Dink said.

"What's the title?" Ruth Rose asked.

They headed toward the Book Nook.

"I don't know," said Dink. "But he wrote in his letter that he's doing some of the research while he's here in Connecticut."

Dink pulled the letter out of his pocket. He read it out loud while he walked.

Dear Mr. Duncan,

Thank you for your kind letter. I'm so impressed that you've read all my books! I have good news. I've made arrangements to come to the Book Nook to sign books. I can use part of my time for research. Thanks for your picture. I'm so happy to finally meet one of my most loyal fans. Short of being kidnapped, nothing will stop me from coming!

See you soon,

Wallis Wallace

The letter was signed Wallis Wallace in loopy letters. Dink grinned. "Pretty neat, huh?"

"Pretty neat, Mister Duncan!" teased Josh.

"You should have that letter framed," Ruth Rose said.

"Great idea!" Dink said.

They passed Howard's Barbershop. Howard waved through his window as they hurried by.

"Come on!" Dink urged as he dragged his friends down the street to the Book Nook.

They looked through the window, out of breath. The bookstore was crowded with kids. The Book Nook's owner, Mr. Paskey, had set up folding chairs. Dink noticed that most of them were already taken.

Dink saw Mr. Paskey sitting behind a table. A big white sign on the table said WELCOME, WALLIS WALLACE!

But the chair behind the sign was empty. Dink gulped and stared at the empty seat.

Where was Wallis Wallace?

Chapter 2

Dink raced into the Book Nook. Josh and Ruth Rose were right behind him. They found three seats behind Tommy Tomko and Eddie Carini.

Dink plopped his pack on the floor. The clock over the cash register said three minutes after eleven.

"Where is he?" Dink whispered to Tommy Tomko.

Tommy turned around. "Beats me. He's not here yet, and Mr. Paskey looks worried."

"What's going on?" Ruth Rose said.

Dink told her and Josh what Tommy had said.

"Paskey does look pretty nervous," Josh whispered.

"Mr. Paskey always looks nervous," Dink whispered back, looking around the room. He saw about thirty kids he knew. Mrs. Davis, Dink's neighbor, was looking at gardening books.

Dink checked out the other grownups in the store. None of them looked like a famous mystery writer.

Mr. Paskey stood up. "Boys and girls, welcome to the Book Nook! Wallis Wallace should be here any second. How many of you have books to be autographed?"

Everyone waved a book in the air.

"Wonderful! I'm sure Wallis Wallace will be happy to know that Green Lawn is a reading town!"

The kids clapped and cheered.

Dink glanced at the clock. Five past eleven. He swallowed, trying to stay calm. Wallis Wallace was late, but it was only by five minutes.

Slowly, five more minutes passed. Dink felt his palms getting damp. Where is Wallis Wallace? he wondered.

Some of the kids started getting restless. Dink heard one kid say, "Whenever I'm late, I get grounded!"

"So where is he?" Josh asked.

Ruth Rose looked at her watch. "It's only ten after," she said. "Famous people are always late."

Now Dink stared at the clock. The big hand jerked forward, paused, then wobbled forward again.

At 11:15, Mr. Paskey stood up again. "I don't understand why Wallis Wallace is late," he said. Dink noticed that his bald head was shiny with sweat. His bow tie was getting a workout.

Mr. Paskey smiled bravely, but his eyes were blinking like crazy through his thick glasses. "Shall we give him a few more minutes?"

The crowd grumbled, but nobody wanted to go anywhere.

Ruth Rose started to read her book. Josh opened his sketch pad and began drawing Mr. Paskey. Dink turned and stared at the door. He mentally ordered

失踪的作家

Wallis Wallace to walk through it. You have to come! thought Dink.

Ever since he had received Wallis Wallace's letter, he'd thought about only one thing: meeting him today.

Suddenly Dink felt his heart skip a beat. THE LETTER! Short of being kidnapped, the letter said, nothing will stop me from coming.

Kidnapped! Dink shook himself. Of course Wallis Wallace hadn't been kidnapped!

Mr. Paskey stood again, but this time he wasn't smiling. "I'm sorry, kids," he said. "But Wallis Wallace doesn't seem to be coming after all."

The kids groaned. They got up, scraping chairs and bumping knees. Mr. Paskey apologized to them as they crowded past, heading for the door.

"I've read every single one of his books," Dink heard Amy Flower tell another girl. "Now I'll probably never meet anyone famous!"

"I can't believe we gave up a soccer game for this!" Tommy Tomko muttered to Eddie Carini on their way out.

Ruth Rose and Josh went next, but Dink remained in his seat. He was too stunned to move.

He felt the letter through his jeans. Short of being kidnapped… Finally Dink got up and walked out.

Josh and Ruth Rose were waiting for him.

"What's the matter?" Ruth Rose said. "You look sick!"

"I am sick," Dink mumbled. "I invited him here. It's all my fault."

"What's all your fault?" Josh asked.

"This!" he said, thrusting the letter into Josh's hands. "Wallis Wallace has been kidnapped!"

Chapter 3

"KIDNAPPED?" Ruth Rose shrieked. Her blue eyes were huge.

Josh and Dink covered their ears.

"Shh!" said Josh. He handed the letter back to Dink and gave a quick gesture with his head. "Some strange woman is watching us!"

Dink had noticed the woman earlier. She'd been sitting in the back of the Book Nook.

"She's coming over here!" Ruth Rose said.

101

The woman had brown hair up in a neat bun. Half-glasses perched on her nose. She was wearing a brown dress and brown shoes, and carried a book bag with a picture of a moose on the side. Around her neck she wore a red scarf covered with tiny black letters.

"Excuse me," she said in a soft, trembly voice. "Did you say Wallis Wallace has been kidnapped?" The woman poked her glasses nervously.

Dink wasn't sure what to say. He thought Wallis Wallace had been kidnapped, but he couldn't be sure. Finally he said, "Well, he might have been."

"My goodness!" gasped the woman.

"Who are you?" Josh asked her.

"Oh, pardon me!" The woman blushed. "My name is Mavis Green," she mumbled. "I'm a writer, and I came to meet Mr. Wallace."

Dink said, "I'm Dink Duncan. These are my friends Ruth Rose and Josh."

Mavis shook hands shyly.

Then she reached into her book bag and pulled out a folded paper.

"Wallis Wallace wrote to me last week. He said something very peculiar in his letter. I didn't think much of it at the time. But when he didn't show up today, and then I heard you mention kidnapping…"

She handed the letter to Dink. Josh and Ruth Rose read it over his shoulder.

Dear Mavis.

Thanks for your note. I'm well, and thank you for asking. But lately my imagination is playing tricks on me. I keep thinking I'm being followed! Maybe that's what happens to mystery writers—we start seeing bad guys in the shadows! At any rate, I'm eager to meet you in Green Lawn, and I look forward to our lunch after the signing.

Wallis Wallace

"Wow!" said Ruth Rose. "First he says he's being followed, and then he winds up missing!"

Dink told Mavis about his letter from Wallis Wallace. "He said the only thing that would keep him from coming today was if he was kidnapped!"

"Oh, dear!" said Mavis. "I just don't understand. Why would anyone want to kidnap Wallis Wallace?"

"If he's the most famous mystery writer in the world, he must be rich, right?" Josh said. "Maybe someone kidnapped him for a ransom!"

Suddenly Josh grabbed Dink and spun him around, pointing toward the street. "Look! The cops are coming! They must have heard about the kidnapping!"

A police officer was walking toward them.

"Josh, that's just Officer Fallon, Jimmy Fallon's grandfather," said Dink. "Jimmy came to get a book signed. I saw him inside the Book Nook."

"Maybe we should show Officer Fallon these letters," Ruth Rose suggested. "They could be clues if Wallis Wallace has really been kidnapped!"

"Who's been kidnapped?" asked Officer Fallon, who was now standing near them. "Not my grandson,

I hope," he added, grinning.

Dink showed Officer Fallon the two letters. "We think Wallis Wallace might have been kidnapped," he said. "He promised he'd come to sign books, but he isn't here."

Officer Fallon read Mavis's letter first, then Dink's. He scratched his chin, then handed the letters back.

"The letters do sound a bit suspicious," he said. "But it's more likely that Mr. Wallace just missed his flight."

Jimmy Fallon ran out of the Book Nook, waving a Wallis Wallace book at his grandfather. "Grampa, he never came! Can we go for ice cream anyway?"

Officer Fallon put a big hand on Jimmy's head. "In a minute, son." To Dink he said, "I wouldn't worry. Mr. Wallace will turn up. Call me tomorrow if there's no news, okay?"

They watched Jimmy and his grandfather walk away.

Dink handed Mavis's letter back to her. He folded his and slid it into his pocket. Crazy thoughts were bouncing around in his head. What if Wallis Wallace really has been kidnapped? It happened because I invited him to Green Lawn. I'm practically an accomplice!

"I don't want to wait till tomorrow," he said finally. "I say we start looking for Wallis Wallace now!"

"Where do we start?" Ruth Rose asked.

Dink jerked his thumb over his shoulder. "Right here at the Book Nook."

"Excuse me," Mavis Green said shyly. "May I come along, too?"

"Sure," Dink said. He marched back inside the Book Nook, with the others following.

Mr. Paskey was putting the Wallis Wallace books back on a shelf. He looked even more nervous than before.

"Excuse me, Mr. Paskey," Dink said. "Have you heard from Wallis Wallace?"

Mr. Paskey's hand shot up to his bow tie. "No, Dink, not a word."

"We think he was kidnapped!" Josh said.

Mr. Paskey swallowed, making his bow tie wiggle. "Now, Joshua, let's not jump to conclusions. I'm sure there's a rational explanation for his absence."

Dink told Mr. Paskey about the two letters. "I'm really worried, Mr. Paskey. Where could he be?"

Mr. Paskey took out a handkerchief and wiped his face. "I have no idea." He removed a paper from his desk and handed it to Dink. "All I have is his itinerary."

The others looked over Dink's shoulder as he read:

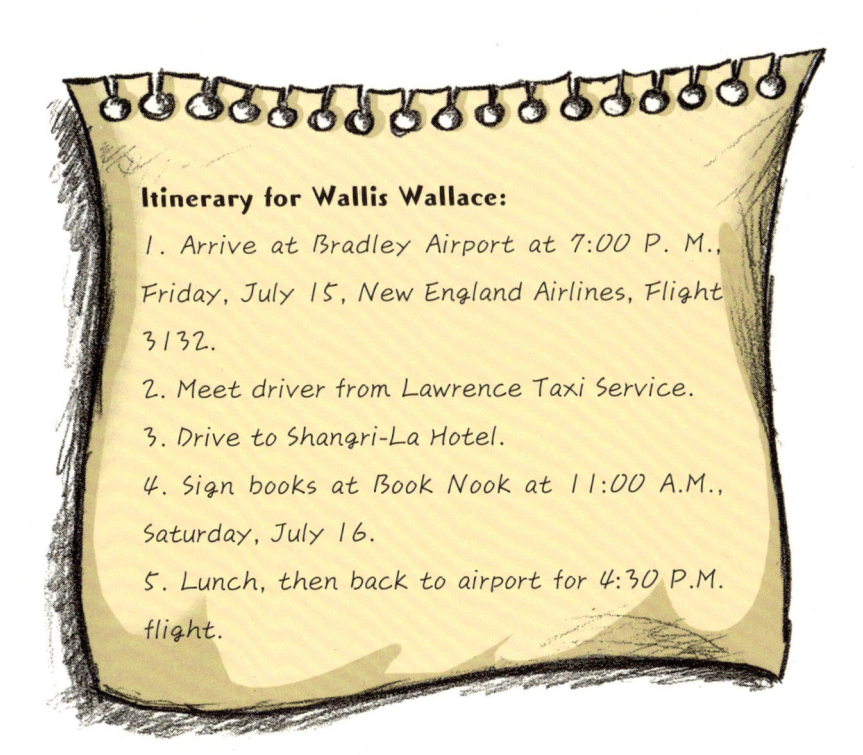

Itinerary for Wallis Wallace:

1. Arrive at Bradley Airport at 7:00 P. M., Friday, July 15, New England Airlines, Flight 3132.
2. Meet driver from Lawrence Taxi Service.
3. Drive to Shangri-La Hotel.
4. Sign books at Book Nook at 11:00 A.M., Saturday, July 16.
5. Lunch, then back to airport for 4:30 P.M. flight.

Mr. Paskey blinked. "Well, I guess that'll be all right. But why do you need the itinerary?"

Dink picked up a marker and drew circles around the words AIRPORT, TAXI, HOTEL, and BOOK NOOK.

"This is like a trail. It leads from the airport last night to the Book Nook today," Dink said. "Somewhere along this trail, Wallis Wallace disappeared."

Dink stared at the itinerary. "And we're going to find him!"

Chapter 4

Mr. Paskey shooed them out of the Book Nook and locked the front door. "I have to eat lunch," he said. He scurried down Main Street.

"Come on," Dink said. "There's a phone in Ellie's Diner."

"Good, we can eat while you're calling..." Josh stopped. "Who are you calling?"

"The airport," Dink said, "to see if Wallis Wallace was on that seven o'clock flight last night."

They walked into Ellie's Diner just as Jimmy Fallon and his grandfather came out. Jimmy was working on a triple-decker chocolate cone.

Ellie stood behind the counter. As usual, her apron was smeared with ketchup, mustard, chocolate, and a lot of stuff Dink didn't recognize.

Ellie smiled. "Hi, Dink. Butter crunch, right?"

Dink shook his head. "No, thanks, Ellie. I came to use the phone."

"Excuse me, but would it be all right if I bought

you each a cone?" Mavis Green asked. "I was going to buy lunch for Mr. Wallace anyway."

"Gee, thanks," Josh said. "I'll have a scoop of mint chip and a scoop of pistachio."

"Oh, you like green ice cream, too," Mavis said. She smiled shyly. "I'll have the same, please."

"I like pink ice cream," Ruth Rose said. "I'll have a

strawberry cone, please. One scoop."

"How about you, Dink?" Mavis asked.

"I'm not hungry, thanks," he said. "But you guys go ahead. I'm going to call the airport."

Dink felt guilty. If he hadn't invited Wallis Wallace to Green Lawn, his favorite author would be safe at home in his castle in Maine.

But Dink couldn't help feeling excited too. He felt like a detective from one of Wallis Wallace's books!

Dink stepped into the phone booth, looked up the number for New England Airlines, and called. When a voice came on, he asked if Wallis Wallace had been aboard Flight 3132 last night.

"He was? Did it land at seven o'clock?" Dink asked. "Thanks a lot!"

He rushed out of the phone booth. "Hey, guys, they told me Wallis Wallace was on the plane—and it landed right on time!"

"So he didn't miss his flight," Ruth Rose said through strawberry-pink lips.

"That's right!" Dink pulled out the itinerary. He drew a line through AIRPORT.

失踪的作家

"This is so exciting!" Ruth Rose said.

"Now what?" Josh asked, working on his double-dipper.

Dink pointed to his next circle on the itinerary. "Now we need to find out if a taxi picked him up," he said.

"Lawrence Taxi is over by the river," Ruth Rose said.

Dink looked at Mavis. "Would you like to come with us? We can walk there in five minutes."

Mavis Green wiped her lips carefully with a napkin. "I'd love to come," she said in her soft voice.

They left Ellie's Diner, walked left on Bridge Lane, then headed down Woodview Road toward the river.

"Mr. Paskey looked pretty upset, didn't he?" Josh said, crunching the last of his cone. His chin was green.

"Wouldn't you be upset if you had a bunch of customers at your store waiting to meet a famous author and he didn't show up?" Ruth Rose asked.

"Yeah, but he was sweating buckets," Josh said. "I wonder if Mr. Paskey kidnapped Wallis Wallace."

113

"Josh, get real! Why would Mr. Paskey kidnap an author?" asked Ruth Rose. "He sells tons of Wallis Wallace's books!"

"I don't think Mr. Paskey is the kidnapper," Dink said. "But in a way, Josh is right. Detectives should consider everyone a suspect, just the way they do in Wallis Wallace's books."

At River Road, they turned left. Two minutes later, Dink pushed open the door of the Lawrence Taxi Service office. He asked the man behind the counter if one of their drivers had met Flight 3132 at Bradley Airport the previous night.

The man ran his finger down a list on a clipboard. "That would be Maureen Higgins. She's out back eating her lunch," he said, pointing over his shoulder. "Walk straight through."

They cut through the building to a grassy area in back. Through the trees, Dink could see the Indian River. The sun reflected off the water like bright coins.

A woman was sitting at a picnic table eating a sandwich and filling in a crossword puzzle.

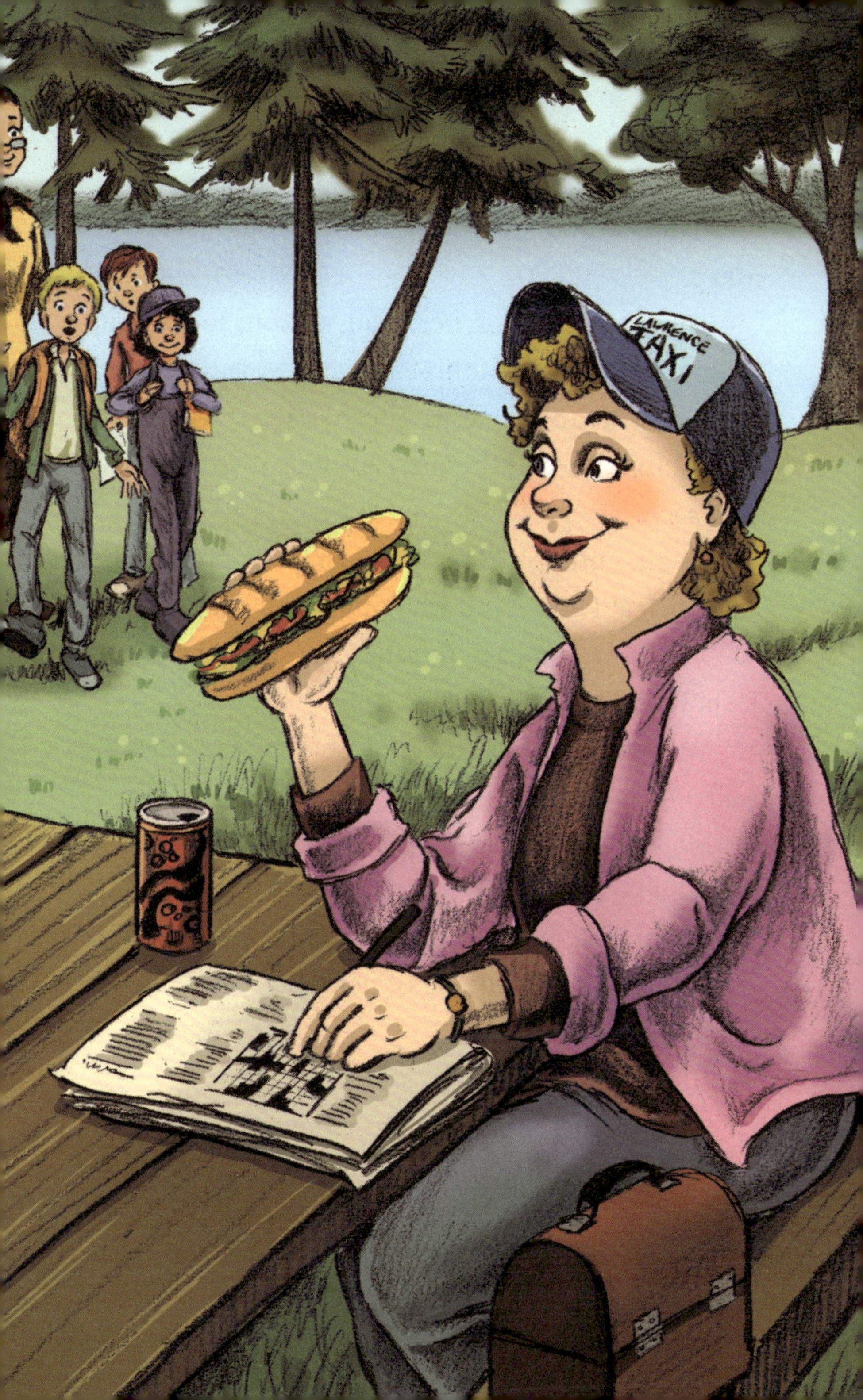
LAURENCE
TAXI

"Excuse me, are you Maureen Higgins?" Dink asked.

The woman shook her head without looking up. "Nope, I'm Marilyn Monroe."

The woman wrote in another letter. Then she looked up. She had the merriest blue eyes Dink had ever seen.

"Yeah, cutie pie, I'm Maureen." She pointed her sandwich at Dink. "And who might you be?"

"I'm Dink Duncan," he said. "These are my friends Josh, Ruth Rose, and Mavis."

"We wondered if you could help us," Ruth Rose said.

Maureen stared at them. "How?"

"Did you pick up a man named Wallis Wallace at the airport last night?" Dink asked.

Maureen squinted one of her blue eyes. "Why do you want to know?"

"Because he's missing!" said Josh.

"Well, I sure ain't got him!" Maureen took a bite out of her sandwich. Mayonnaise oozed onto her fingers.

"I know. I mean, we didn't think you had him," Dink said. "But did you pick him up?"

Maureen nodded, swallowing. "Sure I picked him up. Seven o'clock sharp, I was there with my sign saying WALLACE. The guy spots me, trots over, I take him out to my taxi. He climbs in, carrying a small suitcase. Kinda spooky guy. Dressed in a hat, long raincoat, sunglasses. Sunglasses at night! Doesn't speak a word, just sits. Spooky!"

"Did you take him to the Shangri-la Hotel?" Dink asked.

"Yep. Those were my orders. Guy didn't have to give directions, but it would have been nice if he'd said something. Pass the time, you know? Lotta people, they chat just to act friendly. Not this one. Quiet as a mouse in the back seat."

Maureen wiped mayonnaise from her fingers and lips. "Who is this Wallace fella, anyway?"

"He's a famous writer!" Ruth Rose said.

Maureen's mouth fell open. "You mean I had a celebrity in my cab and never even knew it?"

"What happened when you got to the hotel?" Josh

asked.

Maureen stood up and tossed her napkin into the trash. "I get out of my side, then I open his door. He hops out, hands me a twenty. Last I seen, he's scooting into the lobby."

Dink pulled out the itinerary. He crossed out TAXI with a thick black line. Then he drew a question mark next to HOTEL.

"Thanks a lot, Miss Higgins," he said. "Come on, guys, I have a feeling we're getting closer to finding Wallis Wallace."

Maureen put her hand on Dink's arm. "I just thought of something," she said. "When he handed me my fare, this Wallace fella was smiling."

Dink stared at Maureen. "Smiling?"

She nodded. "Yep. Had a silly grin on his face. Like he knew some big secret or something."

Chapter 5

Back on Main Street, Dink adjusted his backpack and led the way to the Shangri-la Hotel.

"Maureen Higgins said she dropped him off at the hotel last night," he told the others, "so that's our next stop."

"What if she didn't?" Josh said, catching up to Dink.

"What do you mean?"

"I mean maybe Maureen Higgins wasn't telling the truth. Maybe she kidnapped him!"

"And she's hiding him in her lunchbox!" Ruth

Rose said.

"Very funny, Ruth Rose," Josh said. "Maureen Higgins said she drove Wallis Wallace to the hotel. But what if she drove him somewhere else?"

"You could be right," Dink said. "That's why we're going to the hotel."

With Dink in the lead, the four approached the check-in counter in the hotel lobby.

"Excuse me," Dink said to the man behind the counter.

"May we help you?" He was the saddest-looking man Dink had ever seen. He had thin black hair and droopy eyebrows. His skinny mustache looked like a sleeping centipede. A name tag on his suit coat said MR. LINKLETTER.

"We're looking for someone."

Mr. Linkletter stared at Dink.

"He's supposed to be staying in this hotel," Josh said.

The man twitched his mustache at Josh.

"His name is Wallis Wallace," Dink explained. "Can you tell us if he checked in last night?"

Mr. Linkletter patted his mustache. "Young sir, if we had such a guest, we wouldn't give out any information. We have rules at the Shangri-la," he added in a deep, sad voice.

"But he's missing!" Ruth Rose said. "He was supposed to be at the Book Nook this morning and he never showed up!"

Dink pulled out the itinerary. "See, he was coming here from the airport. The taxi driver said she saw him walk into this lobby."

"And he's famous!" Ruth Rose said. She placed her book on the counter in front of Mr. Linkletter. "He wrote this!"

Sighing, Mr. Linkletter looked down at Ruth Rose. "We are quite aware of who Mr. Wallace is, young miss."

Mr. Linkletter turned his sad eyes back on Dink. He flipped through the hotel register, glanced at it, then quickly shut the book. "Yes, Mr. Wallace checked in," he said. "He arrived at 8:05."

"He did? What happened after that?" Dink asked.

Mr. Linkletter pointed toward a bank of elevators.

"He went to his room. We offered to have his suitcase carried, but he preferred to do it himself."

"Have you seen Mr. Wallace yet today?" Mavis asked.

"No, madam, I haven't seen him. Mr. Wallace is still in his room."

Still in his room!

Suddenly Dink felt relieved. He felt a little foolish, too. Wallis Wallace hadn't been kidnapped after all. He was probably in his room right now!

"Can you call him?" Dink asked.

Mr. Linkletter tapped his fingers on the closed hotel register. He patted his mustache and squinted his eyes at Dink.

"Please?" Dink said. "We just want to make sure he's okay."

Finally Mr. Linkletter turned around. He stepped a few feet away and picked up a red telephone.

As soon as his back was turned, Josh grabbed the hotel register. He quickly found yesterday's page. Dink and the others crowded around Josh for a peek.

Dink immediately recognized Wallis Wallace's

signature, scrawled in big loopy letters. He had checked in to Room 303 at five after eight last night.

Dink pulled out his letter from Wallis Wallace and compared the two signatures. They were exactly the same.

Josh dug his elbow into Dink's side. "Look!" he whispered.

Josh was pointing at the next line in the register.

ROOM 302 had been printed there. Check-in time was 8:15.

"Someone else checked in right after Wallis Wallace!" Ruth Rose whispered.

"But the signature is all smudged," Dink said. "I can't read the name."

When Mr. Linkletter hung up the phone, Josh shoved the register away.

As Mr. Linkletter turned back around, Dink shut the register. He looked up innocently. "Is he in his room?" Dink asked.

"I don't know." Mr. Linkletter tapped his fingers on his mustache. "There was no answer."

Dink's stomach dropped. His mind raced.

If Wallis Wallace had checked into his room last night, why hadn't he shown up at the Book Nook today?

And why wasn't he answering his phone?

Maybe Wallis Wallace had been kidnapped after all!

Chapter 6

Dink stared at Mr. Linkletter. "No answer? Are you sure?"

Mr. Linkletter nodded. He looked puzzled. "Perhaps he's resting and doesn't want to be disturbed."

"Can we go up and see?" Ruth Rose smiled sweetly at Mr. Linkletter. "Then we'd know for sure."

Mr. Linkletter shook his head. "We cannot disturb our guests, young miss. We have rules at the Shangri-la. Now good day, and thank you."

Ruth Rose opened her mouth. "But, Mis—"

"Good day," Mr. Linkletter said firmly again.

Dink and the others walked toward the door.

"Something smells fishy," muttered Dink.

"Yeah," Josh said, "and I think it's that Linkletter guy. See how he tried to hide the register? Then he turned his back. Maybe he didn't even call Room 303. Maybe he was warning his partners in crime!"

"What are you suggesting, Josh?" Mavis asked.

"Maybe Mr. Linkletter is the kidnapper," Josh said. "He was the last one to see Wallis Wallace."

A man wearing a red cap tapped Dink on the shoulder. "Excuse me, but I overheard you talking to my boss, Mr. Linkletter. Maybe I can help you find Wallis Wallace. My kids love his books."

"Great!" Dink said. "Can you get us into his room?"

The man shook his head. "No, but I know the maid who cleaned the third-floor rooms this morning. Maybe she noticed something."

With his back to Mr. Linkletter, the man scribbled a few words on a pad and handed the page to Dink. "Good luck!" the man whispered, and hurried away.

"What'd he write?" Josh asked.

"Outside," Dink said.

They all shoved through the revolving door. In

失踪的作家

front of the hotel, Dink looked at the piece of paper. "The maid's name is Olivia Nugent. She lives at the Acorn Apartments, Number Four."

"Livvy Nugent? I know her!" Ruth Rose said. "She used to be my baby-sitter."

"The Acorn is right around the corner on Oak Street," Dink said. "Let's go!"

Soon all four were standing in front of Livvy Nugent's door. She answered it with a baby in her arms. Another little kid held on to her leg and stared at Dink and the others. He had peanut butter all over his face and in his hair.

"Hi," the boy's mother said. "I'm not buying any cookies and I already get the *Green Lawn Gazette*." She was wearing a man's blue shirt and jeans. Her brown hair stuck out from under a Yankees baseball cap.

"Livvy, it's me!" Ruth Rose said.

Olivia stared at Ruth Rose, then broke into a grin.

"Ruth Rose, you're so big! What are you up to these days?"

"A man at the hotel gave us your name."

127

"What man?"

"He was sort of old, wearing a red cap," Dink said.

Livvy chuckled. "Freddy old? He's only thirty! So why did he send you to see me?"

"He told us you cleaned the rooms on the third floor this morning," Dink said. "Did you clean Room 303?"

失踪的作家

Livvy Nugent shifted the baby to her other arm. "Randy, please stop pulling on Mommy's leg. Why don't you go finish your lunch?" Randy ran back into the apartment.

"No," Livvy told Dink. "Nobody slept in that room. The bed was still made this morning. The towels were still clean and dry. I remember because there were two rooms in a row that I didn't have to clean— 303 and 302. Room 302 had a Do Not Disturb sign hanging on the doorknob. So I came home early, paid off the baby-sitter, and made our lunches."

"But Mr. Linkletter told us Wallis Wallace checked into Room 303 last night," Ruth Rose said.

"Not the Wallis Wallace? The mystery writer? My kid sister devours his books!"

Dink nodded. "He was supposed to sign books at the Book Nook this morning. But he never showed up!"

"We even saw his signature on the hotel register," Ruth Rose said.

"Well, Wallis Wallace might have signed in, but he never slept in that room." Livvy grinned. "Unless he's

129

a ghost."

"I wonder if Mr. Linkletter could have made a mistake about the room number," Mavis suggested quietly.

Livvy smiled at Mavis. "You must not be from around here. Mr. Linkletter never makes mistakes."

"So Wallis Wallace signed in, but he didn't sleep in his room," said Dink. "That means…"

"Someone must have kidnapped him before he went to bed!" Josh said.

Livvy's eyes bugged. "Kidnapped! Geez, Mr. Linkletter will have a fit." She imitated his voice. "We have rules about kidnappings at the Shangri-la!"

Everyone except Dink laughed. All he could think about was Wallis Wallace, his favorite author, kidnapped.

Suddenly a crash came from inside the apartment. "Oops, gotta run," Livvy said. "Randy is playing bulldozer with his baby sister's stroller again. I hope you find Wallis Wallace. My kid sister will die if he doesn't write another book!"

They walked slowly back to Main Street. Dink felt

as though his brain was spinning around inside his head.

Now he felt certain that Wallis Wallace had been kidnapped.

But who did it? And when?

And where was Wallis Wallace being kept?

"Guys, I'm feeling confused," he said. "Can we just sit somewhere and go over the facts again?"

"Good idea," Josh said. "I always think better when I'm eating."

"I'm feeling a bit peckish, too," Mavis said. "I need a quiet cup of tea and a sandwich. Should we meet again after lunch?"

Ruth Rose looked at her watch. "Let's meet at two o'clock."

"Where?" Josh asked.

"Back at the hotel." Dink peered through the door glass at Mr. Linkletter.

"Unless Maureen Higgins and Mr. Linkletter are both lying," he said, "Wallis Wallace walked into the Shangri-la last night—and never came out."

Chapter 7

Dink, Josh, and Ruth Rose left Mavis at Ellie's Diner, then headed for Dink's house. Dink made tuna sandwiches and lemonade. Ruth Rose brought a bag of potato chips and some raisin cookies from her house next door.

They ate at the picnic table in Dink's backyard. Dink took a bite of his sandwich. After he swallowed, he said, "Let's go over what we know."

He moved his lemonade glass to the middle of the table. "My glass is the airport," he said. "We know Wallis Wallace landed."

失踪的作家

"How do we know he did?" Josh asked.

"The airport told me the plane landed, Josh."

"And Maureen Higgins said she picked him up," Ruth Rose added.

"Okay, so your glass is the airport," Josh said. "Keep going, Dink."

Dink slid his sandwich plate over next to his glass. "My plate is Maureen's taxi." He put a cookie on the plate. "The cookie is Wallis Wallace getting into the taxi."

Dink slid the plate over to the opened potato chip bag. "This bag is the hotel." He walked the Wallis Wallace cookie from the plate into the bag.

Dink looked at Josh and Ruth Rose. "But what happened to Wallis Wallace after he walked into the lobby?"

"I'll tell you what happened," Josh said. He lined up four cookies in a row. "This little cookie is Mr. Paskey. These three are Maureen, Mr. Linkletter, and Olivia Nugent."

Josh looked up and waggled his eyebrows. "I think these four cookies planned the kidnapping together!"

Ruth Rose laughed. "Josh, Mr. Paskey and Livvy

133

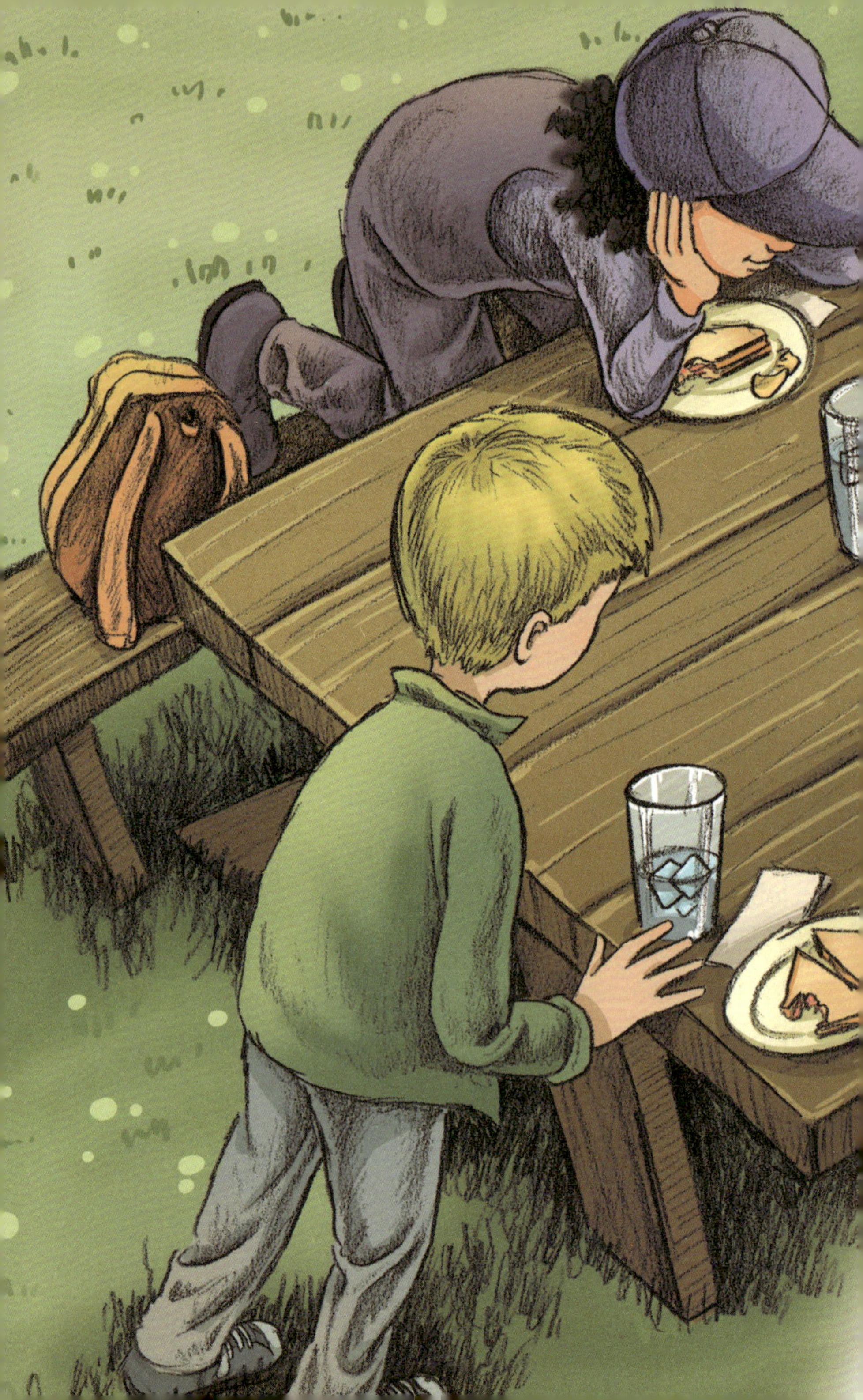

Nugent are friends of ours. Do you really think they planned this big kidnapping? And can you see Mr. Linkletter and my baby-sitter pulling off a kidnapping together?"

Josh ate a potato chip. "Well, maybe not. But someone kidnapped the guy!"

"Our trail led us to the hotel, and then it ended," Dink said. "What I want to know is, if Wallis Wallace isn't in his room, where is he?"

Dink nibbled on a cookie thoughtfully. "I'm getting a headache trying to sort it all out."

Ruth Rose dug in Dink's backpack and brought out three Wallis Wallace books. "I have an idea." She handed books to Dink and Josh and kept one.

"What're these for?" Dink asked.

"Josh made me think of something Wallis Wallace wrote in *The Mystery in the Museum*," Ruth Rose said. "He said the more you know about the victim, the easier it is to figure out who did the crime."

She turned to the back cover of her book. "So let's try to find out more about our victim. Listen to this." She started reading out loud. "When not writing, the author likes to work in the garden. Naturally, Wallis Wallace's favorite color is green."

"Fine," said Josh, "but how does knowing his favorite color help us find him, Ruth Rose?"

"I don't know, but maybe if we read more about him, we'll discover some clues," Ruth Rose said. "What does it say on the back of your book?"

Josh flipped the book over and began reading. "Wallis Wallace lives in a castle called Moose Manor." He looked up. "We already knew he lived in a castle. I don't see any clues yet, you guys."

Ruth Rose stared at Josh. "You know, something is bugging me, but I can't figure out what it is. Something someone said today, maybe." She shook her head. "Anyway, read yours, Dink."

Dink read from the back cover of his book. "Wallis Wallace gives money from writing books to help preserve the wild animals that live in Maine."

"Okay, he gives money away to save animals, lives in a castle, and grows a bunch of green stuff," Josh said, counting on his fingers. "Still no clues."

Josh took another cookie. "But I just thought of something." He began slowly munching on the cookie.

Dink raised his eyebrows. "Are you going to tell us, Josh?"

"Well, I was thinking about Room 302. Remember, someone signed the register right after Wallis Wallace

137

checked into Room 303? And the signature was all smudged? And then Olivia Nugent—"

"—told us that Room 302 had a Do Not Disturb sign on it!" Ruth Rose interrupted. "Livvy never went into that room at all!"

Just then Dink's mother drove up the driveway. She got out of the car, waved, and started walking toward the picnic table.

"Oh, no!" Dink said. "If Mom finds out I'm trying to find a kidnapper, she won't let me out of the house! Don't say anything, okay?"

"Can't I even say hi?" Josh asked.

Dink threw a potato chip at Josh. "Say hi, then shut up about you-know-what!"

"Hi, Mrs. Duncan!" Josh said, sliding a look at Dink.

"Hi, kids. How was the book signing? Tell me all about Wallis Wallace, Dink. Is he as wonderful as you expected?"

Dink stared at his mother. He didn't want to lie. But if he told her the truth, she wouldn't let him keep looking for Wallis Wallace. And Dink had a sudden feeling that they were very close to finding him.

We can't stop now! he thought. He looked at his mother and grinned stupidly.

"Dink? Honey? Why is your mouth open?"

He closed his mouth. Think, Dink! he ordered himself.

Suddenly Josh knocked over his lemonade glass. The sticky cold liquid spilled into Dink's lap.

Dink let out a yowl and jumped up.

"Gee, sorry!" said Josh.

"Paper towels to the rescue!" Dink's mother ran toward the house.

"Good thinking, Josh," Dink said, wiping at his wet jeans. "But did you have to spill it on me? You had the whole yard!"

Josh grinned. "Some people are never satisfied. I got you out of hot water, didn't I?"

"Right into cold lemonade," Ruth Rose said.

Dink blotted his jeans with a handful of paper napkins. "Come on. Let's go meet Mavis before my mom comes back. There's something weird happening on the third floor of the Shangri-la!"

Chapter 8

Dink's jeans were nearly dry by the time they reached the hotel. Mavis was waiting out front.

"How was your lunch?" she asked timidly.

"Fine, thanks," Dink said. "We talked it over, and we think there's something fishy going on on the third floor of this hotel."

Suddenly Mavis began coughing. She held up her scarf in front of her mouth.

Dink noticed that the letters on the scarf were tiny M's. "Are you okay?" he asked.

"Should I run in and get you some water?" asked Josh.

Mavis took off her glasses and shook her head. "No, I'm fine, thank you. Dear me, I don't know what happened! Now, what were you saying about the third floor?"

"We think Wallis Wallace may be up there," Ruth Rose said. She reminded Mavis about the smudged signature for Room 302 and the Do Not Disturb sign on the door.

Mavis replaced her eyeglasses. "Mercy! What do you think we should do?"

"Follow me!" Dink said. For the second time, they all trooped into the hotel lobby.

Mr. Linkletter watched them from behind the counter.

"Hi," Dink said. "Remember us?"

"Vividly," Mr. Linkletter said.

"Wallis Wallace checked into Room 303, right?"

"That is correct," said Mr. Linkletter.

"Well, we talked to the maid who cleaned that room," Dink went on. "She told us no one slept in it."

"You spoke to Olivia Nugent? When? How?"

"We have our ways," Josh said.

A to Z 神秘案件

"So," Dink went on, "we think Wallis Wallace disappeared right here in this hotel."

"And Wallis Wallace is a very famous writer," Ruth Rose reminded Mr. Linkletter. "Millions of kids are waiting to read his next book," she added sweetly.

Mr. Linkletter's sad eyes grew large. He swallowed and his Adam's apple bobbed up and down. He rubbed his forehead as though he had a headache.

Then Dink told Mr. Linkletter about Room 302. "Miss Nugent said there was a Do Not Disturb sign on the door."

Ruth Rose pointed to the register. "See? The signature is all smudged!"

"We think the kidnappers are hiding Wallis Wallace in that room!" Josh said.

At the word "kidnappers," Mr. Linkletter closed

A to Z 神秘案件

his eyes. He opened a drawer, took out a bottle of headache pills, and put one on his tongue.

"Just to be on the safe side, perhaps we should check both rooms, Mr. Linkletter," Mavis said quietly.

"It'll just take a minute," Dink said.

Mr. Linkletter let out a big sigh. "Very well, but this is most unusual. Things run very smoothly at the Shangri-la."

They all got into the elevator. No one spoke. Dink watched Mr. Linkletter jiggling his bunch of keys. Mr. Linkletter kept his eyes on the little arrow telling them which floor they were on.

The elevator door opened on the third floor. Mr. Linkletter unlocked Room 303. "Most unusual," he muttered.

The room was empty and spotlessly clean. "Strange, very strange," Mr. Linkletter said.

They moved to Room 302, where a Do Not Disturb sign still hung on the door knob.

Mr. Linkletter knocked. They all leaned toward the door.

"Listen, I hear a voice!" Josh said.

"What's it saying?" Ruth Rose asked.

Then they all heard it.

The voice was muffled, but it was definitely yelling, "HELP!"

Chapter 9

Mr. Linkletter unlocked the door and shoved it open.

A man with curly blond hair stared back at them. He was sitting in a chair with his feet tied in front of him. His arms were tied behind his back. A towel was wrapped around his mouth.

"Oh, my goodness!" Mr. Linkletter cried.

Everyone rushed into the room.

Dink ran behind the chair to untie the man's hands while Josh untied his feet.

Mavis unwrapped the towel from around his face.

"Thank goodness you got here!" the man said. "I'm

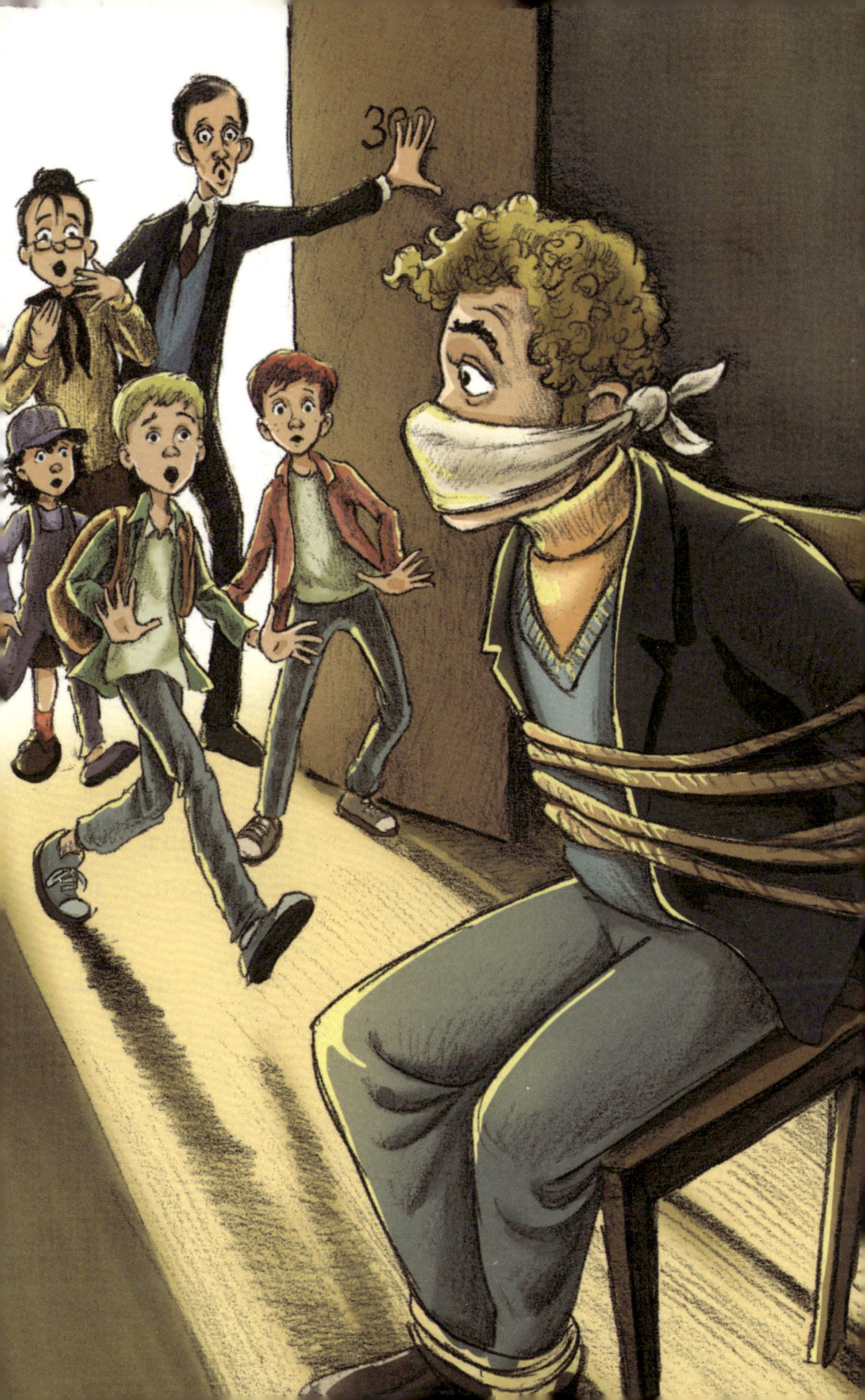

A to Z 神秘案件

Wallis Wallace. Someone knocked on my door last night. A voice said he was from room service. When I opened the door, two men dragged me in here and tied me up."

He looked at Dink. "You're Dink Duncan! I recognize you from the picture you sent. How did you find me?"

"We followed your itinerary," Dink said. He showed Mr. Wallace the sheet of paper. "We got it from Mr. Paskey and used it as a trail. The trail led us to this room!"

"I'm so sorry I missed the book signing," Wallis Wallace said. "As you can see, I was a bit tied up."

He smiled. Then he rubbed his jaw. "My mouth is sore from that towel. I can't believe I was kidnapped! And I can't wait to get back to my safe little cottage in Maine."

"Can you describe the two guys who kidnapped you?" Dink asked. "We should tell Officer Fallon so he can try to find them."

Wallis Wallace stared at Dink. "The two guys? Oh…well, um, I don't think I'll—"

"HEY!" Ruth Rose suddenly yelled.

Everyone looked at her.

"What's the matter?" asked Dink. "You look funny, Ruth Rose."

Ruth Rose was staring at the red scarf draped around Mavis's neck. She pointed at the man who'd been tied up. "You're not Wallis Wallace!"

Then she looked at Mavis Green. "You are," she said quietly.

Chapter 10

"Ruth Rose, what are you talking about?" Josh said.

Dink didn't know what to think except that he was getting a headache.

"What makes you think I'm Wallis Wallace?" Mavis asked.

Ruth Rose walked over to Mavis. "May I borrow your scarf?" she said.

Ruth Rose held the scarf up so everyone could see it. "When I first saw this scarf, I thought these little black letters were M's," she said. "M for Mavis."

She looked at Mavis Green. "But they're not M's,

are they?"

She turned the scarf completely upside down. "What do they look like now?"

Dink stepped closer. "They're little W's now!"

"Right. Double-U, double-U for Wallis Wallace!" Ruth Rose pointed at the man. "You just said you live in a little cottage. But Wallis Wallace lives in a big castle in Maine. It says so on the cover of *The Silent Swamp*."

Ruth Rose pointed at Mavis's book bag. "Seeing your bag again made me remember something I thought of today. Josh read that your castle was called Moose Manor. There's a picture of a moose on the side of your bag."

Ruth Rose handed the scarf back to Mavis. "And we read that Wallis Wallace's favorite color is green. You like green ice cream, and you chose Mavis Green for your fake name."

Everyone was staring at Ruth Rose, except for the man they had untied. He started laughing.

"The cat's out of the bag now, sis," he said.

Then Mavis laughed and gave Ruth Rose a hug.

"Yes, Ruth Rose," Mavis said. "I really am Wallis Wallace." She put her hand on the man's shoulder. "And this is my brother, Walker Wallace. We've been planning my 'kidnapping' for weeks!"

Dink stared at Mavis, or whoever she was. "You mean Wallis Wallace is a woman?" he said.

"Yes, Dink, I'm a woman, and I'm definitely Wallis Wallace." She winked at him. "Honest!"

Mavis, the real Wallis Wallace, sat on the bed. She took off her glasses and pulled the barrettes out of her hair. She shook her hair until it puffed out in a mass of wild curls.

"Thank goodness I can be myself now!" she said. "All day I've had to act like timid Mavis Green. I can't wait to get out of this fuddy-duddy dress and into my jeans again!"

She kicked off her shoes and wiggled her toes in the air. "Boy, does that feel good!"

Dink blinked and shook his head. Mavis Green was really Wallis Wallace? He couldn't believe it. "But why did you pretend to be kidnapped?" he asked.

The real Wallis Wallace grinned at the kids'

surprised faces. "I owe you an explanation," she said.

"My new book is about a children's mystery writer who gets kidnapped. In my book, some children rescue the writer. I wanted to find out how real kids might solve the mystery," she explained.

She smiled at Dink. "Then your letter came, inviting me to Green Lawn. That's what gave me the idea to fake my own kidnapping. I'd become Mavis Green and watch what happened."

"Oh, yeah!" Dink said. "In your letter, you said you were doing some research in Connecticut."

She nodded. "Yes, and I mentioned the word 'kidnap' in the letter to get you thinking along those lines." She smiled at the three kids. "I thought I'd have to give you more clues, but you solved the mystery all by yourselves!"

Dink laughed. "You recognized me in the bookstore from my picture," he said. "And you didn't send me a picture so I wouldn't recognize you!"

"Then my nutty sister dragged me into her plan," Walker Wallace said. "I should be home checking my lobster pots."

"While you were eating lunch, Walker and I ate ours up here," Wallis said. "Then, just before two o'clock, I tied him in the chair and ran downstairs to meet you out front as Mavis."

Wallis Wallace threw back her head and laughed. "Do you remember downstairs when Dink said there was something fishy on the third floor?"

She got up and stood next to her brother. "Well, I'm always teasing Walker about smelling fishy from handling his lobster bait. So when you said something was fishy in the hotel, I had to pretend to cough so you wouldn't know I was really laughing!"

"Boy, did you have us fooled," Dink said.

Wallis Wallace grinned. "Mr. Paskey was in on it. I had to tell him the truth. As you saw this morning at the Book Nook, my little scheme made him very nervous. I've promised him I'll come back and do a real book signing soon. But I'll be in disguise, so be prepared for anything!"

Dink shook his head. "I was so disappointed because I couldn't meet my favorite author this morning," he said. "And I've been with you all day and didn't even know it!"

She looked at Dink. "I'm so sorry I tricked you. Will you forgive me?"

Dink blushed. "Sure."

"I have a question," Josh said. "Where did you really sleep last night?"

"Right here in Room 302. A few weeks ago, I telephoned to reserve two rooms next to each other. Last night, I checked into Room 303 as Wallis Wallace, the man. Up in Room 303, I took off the hat and coat and sunglasses. Then I sneaked back down to the lobby wearing a blond wig. I checked in again, this time into Room 302."

"Did you smudge the signature?" Ruth Rose asked.

"Oh, you noticed that!" Wallis said. "I'm so used to signing my real name in books, I started to write Wallis. So I 'accidentally' smudged it."

"I have a question, Mavis, I mean Miss Wallace. what should we call you?" Dink asked.

"My friends call me Wallis," she said.

"Well, the taxi driver told us you were smiling in the taxi. What were you smiling about?"

Wallis Wallace was smiling now. "Oh, about a lot of things. First, I was wearing a man's disguise, and that made me feel pretty silly. And I knew I was going to meet you, one of my biggest fans. And I was happy because I knew whatever happened, the next day would be fun!"

"I sure had fun," Josh said, grinning, "Poor Mr. Paskey, having to lie to everyone with a straight face!"

"Boy, did I have a hard time pretending to be Mavis all day," Wallis said. "But my plan worked. I met three brilliant detectives. You helped me to see how real kids would investigate a kidnapping. Now I can go back to Maine and finish my book."

"How come your book jackets never say that you're a woman?" Ruth Rose asked.

Wallis Wallace smiled. "Because of my name, most people assume that I'm a man," she explained. "I let them think that so I can do my research easier. I've learned that people clam up if they know I'm Wallis Wallace. So out in public I pretend I'm Mavis Green, just a regular person, not a mystery writer."

"I get it!" Dink said. "You don't have your picture on your books so people can't recognize you."

"Right. And I hope you'll keep my secret."

"We will. Right, guys?" Ruth Rose said.

"Thank you! Any more questions?" Wallis asked.

失踪的作家

"Yeah," Walker said, giving his sister a look. "When do we leave? I've got lobsters waiting for me."

"I have a question, too," Dink said. "Will you send me your picture now?"

"Yes, but I'll do better than that," Wallis said. "I'll dedicate my next book to my three new friends!"

Dink, Josh, and Ruth Rose did a triple high five.

"Excuse me," Mr. Linkletter said from the door where he had been standing.

They all looked at him.

"It's nearly checkout time."

Everyone laughed.

Mr. Linkletter smiled, but just a little.

Text copyright © 1997 by Ron Roy
Cover art copyright © 2015 by Stephen Gilpin
Interior illustrations copyright © 1997 by John Steven Gurney
All rights reserved. Published in the United States by Random House Children's Books,
a division of Random House LLC, a Penguin Random House Company, New York.
Originally published in paperback by Random House Children's Books, New York, in 1997.

本书中英双语版由中南博集天卷文化传媒有限公司与企鹅兰登（北京）文化发展有限公司合作出版。

"企鹅"及其相关标识是企鹅兰登已经注册或尚未注册的商标。
未经允许，不得擅用。
封底凡无企鹅防伪标识者均属未经授权之非法版本。

©中南博集天卷文化传媒有限公司。本书版权受法律保护。未经权利人许可，任何人不得以任何方式使用本书包括正文、插图、封面、版式等任何部分内容，违者将受到法律制裁。

著作权合同登记号：字18-2023-258

图书在版编目（CIP）数据

失踪的作家：汉英对照／（美）罗恩·罗伊著；（美）约翰·史蒂文·格尼绘；高芸译. -- 长沙：湖南少年儿童出版社，2024.10. -- （A to Z神秘案件）.
ISBN 978-7-5562-7817-6
Ⅰ.H319.4
中国国家版本馆CIP数据核字第20241VL997号

A TO Z SHENMI ANJIAN SHIZONG DE ZUOJIA

A to Z神秘案件 失踪的作家

［美］罗恩·罗伊 著　［美］约翰·史蒂文·格尼 绘　高芸 译

责任编辑：唐凌 李炜	策划出品：李炜 张苗苗 文赛峰
策划编辑：文赛峰	特约编辑：张晓璐
营销编辑：付佳 杨朔 周晓茜	封面设计：霍雨佳
版权支持：王媛媛	版式设计：马睿君
插图上色：河北传图文化	内文排版：马睿君

出 版 人：刘星保
出　　版：湖南少年儿童出版社
地　　址：湖南省长沙市晚报大道89号
邮　　编：410016
电　　话：0731-82196320
常年法律顾问：湖南崇民律师事务所　柳成柱律师
经　　销：新华书店
开　　本：875 mm×1230 mm　1/32
字　　数：87千字
版　　次：2024年10月第1版
书　　号：ISBN 978-7-5562-7817-6
印　　刷：三河市中晟雅豪印务有限公司
印　　张：5
印　　次：2024年10月第1次印刷
定　　价：280.00元（全10册）

若有质量问题，请致电质量监督电话：010-59096394　团购电话：010-59320018